Thrifty Traveler's guide to Costa Rica

A Perfect Journey for the Budget Traveler

Visit the Best Surfing, Ecotourism, Nature, Food & Lodging Recommendations by a Seasoned Traveler

By

Jasmine Ayla

Thames & Tower
PUBLISHING PRESS

Cover Designer & Art Director

Rebecca Johnson

1st Edition

Contents

About the Author

Jasmine Ayla is a freelance writer, editor, and content creator based out of Maui, Hawai'i, USA.

Jasmine enjoys traveling the world, taking photos, writing, surfing and hiking.

You can read more of her writing and about her adventures at www.jewelsoftheearthandsea.net.

Please note that all of the photos used in this manuscript were produced by Jasmine Ayla and may not be copied or reproduced without written permission from the author or publisher. Thank you for respecting digital copyright.

Please leave a review online where you purchased this book as online reviews help me reach more readers. Thank you in advance!

Introduction

Right in the middle of the giant continents of North and South America lies a relatively small, thin belt of land joining the two landmasses: Central America. The belt of Central America is bordered by the sparkling sea of the Caribbean to the east and the ancient waters of the Pacific Ocean to the west. Nestled right in the middle of the "belt" is the country of Costa Rica, the country of Nicaragua to the north, and the country of Panama to the south.

If you've ever dreamed of visiting Costa Rica one day, this book is for you. The name "Costa Rica" translates to "Rich Coast" in Spanish, a perfect term for the treasure you will find along its hundreds of miles of stunning coastlines running alongside the Caribbean Sea and the Pacific Ocean. But this tropical nation offers much, much more than its beaches. In fact, it is brimming with beauty and adventure around every corner, with a surprising amount of biodiversity. A traveler will be delighted to discover that Costa Rica boasts no less than 12 microclimates ranging from hot humidity to cold and frosty, and everything in between. The largely tropical country features a multitude of white sand, black sand, and shell beaches. Further inland exists a fabulous variety of landscapes: cloud rainforests, towering volcanic mountain ranges, grassy plains, rolling hills, waterfalls, rivers - you name it, Costa Rica's probably got it.

On top of that, Costa Rica is famous for its incredibly friendly locals, great food with many healthy options, amazing diving, snorkeling, surfing, and hiking. In short, this tiny country has everything a tropical dream should.

Oftentimes, being a budget traveler means that you have to forego a few of your destination's biggest attractions to stay within your budget, not so in this friendly little country. There are two very important and unique features of a holiday à la Costa Rica. First, it's one of the most sustainably governed and eco-friendly countries on Earth - so you will leave as small of a carbon footprint as possible while supporting sustainability and the local economy. Second, even with all of the unique, beautiful offerings, you will find here, you can still plan a great budget vacation while enjoying the best the country has to offer!

Here are some quick facts about Costa Rica:

> The nation of Costa Rica is officially known as the Republic of Costa Rica ("República de Costa Rica" in Spanish).
>
> Costa Rica has a population of about 5 million people (as of 2020).
>
> The population is largely centered in the country's capital city, San José (330,000), and the surrounding metropolitan area (2 million). The rest of the population (2,670,000) is scattered throughout the lovely, varied countryside, with the majority concentrated along the coastlines.
>
> The country has a land area of approximately 20,000 square miles (or 51,000 square kilometers). For comparison, it's a little bit smaller than the U.S. state of West Virginia and the European country of Ireland.

A crucial part of any vacation-planning is the research. I've spent years visiting this lovely little country, and it's easily my favorite destination on the planet! Trust me when I say that it's my pleasure to compile my favorite facts about Costa Rica and the best vacation advice for you when you visit. Warning: there's so much to see and do in this tropical nation that to cover it all, this book would have had to have 1,000s of pages - so keep in mind, this is just a summary of the highlights, and by no means conclusive. Continue reading to discover my ten top nuggets of informational gold to help you get the most joy out of your beautiful trip while easily maintaining a budget!

A Brief, Fascinating History of Costa Rica

The First Signs of Human Life

The first evidence of human settlement discovered in Costa Rica, by the Reventazón River, is believed to date all the way back to 10,000 BC, or about 12,000 years ago. This is quite a bit earlier than originally believed, and for a good reason - it is the oldest evidence of human life discovered anywhere in the area. That means that Costa Rica is one of the oldest settlements of human life in Central America, a pretty amazing claim to fame!

Between 10,000 BC and the arrival of the Europeans in the 15th century, Costa Rica was called home by dozens of indigenous groups, each with its own unique culture and way of life. These natives were hunters and gatherers living peacefully, with the Costa Rica region serving as an intermediate area, or middle ground, between the native Mesoamerican and Andean cultures.

The Arrival of the Europeans

According to common history, Christopher Columbus was the first European to set eyes on Costa Rica, or "Rich Coast" as the literal translation goes. "Christopher Colombus" is an anglicized version of this Italian explorer's name, though - his real name was Cristoforo Colombo. On his fourth and final voyage to the Americas, Columbo dropped anchor at Puerto Limón on the Caribbean coast one fateful day in 1502. The country would forever be changed, just like every other country in Central America was eventually influenced by the power and control of faraway Spain. Columbo and his men saw the gold rings worn in the noses and on the fingers of local Caribbean natives and mistakenly assumed that Costa Rica was a land of golden riches to be plundered - hence the name, "Rich Coast." Columbus and his men overcame the natives by force, and in 1524, he unilaterally incorporated the Costa Rican territory into the Captaincy General of

Guatemala, which itself was a subdivision of the Viceroyalty of New Spain (Mexico). For the next 300 years, Costa Ricans and their country would be a neglected colony under the rule of Spain.

Unfortunately for the conquistadores, or Spanish conquerors, there was little to no gold to be found in the territory. As a result, the small country slowly languished into becoming a "backwater" province of Spanish territory, of little importance due to the supposed lack of riches. The native people suffered from minimal development and poverty during this time, along with the inevitable slavery, genocide, and disease found elsewhere in territories conquered by the Spanish. Along with the conquistadores, treasure-hunters, and settlers, the majority of indigenous people died during this difficult time.

The War of Independence with Spain

As a consequence of Mexico's victory in the Mexican War of Independence from Spain, which lasted from 1810 until September 15, 1821, Guatemala, along with Costa Rica and the other nations of Central America, became individual states in an independent Central American empire free of Spain's rule. The new empire was called the Federal Republic of Central America and was ruled from Guatemala, and later El Salvador. In a strange happenstance because of their remote location, Costa Ricans were informed of their independence from Spain an entire month after Guatemala knew; however, they still proudly celebrate their Independence Day on September 15.

Over the next two years, there was an uncertainty in Costa Rica between the "Imperialists" (who supported Costa Rica joining the country of Mexico) and the "Republicans" (who supported Costa Rica's absolute independence). This tension resulted in the Battle of Ochomogo in April 1823, where the Republicans won, and Costa Rica did not join Mexico. It would take another 15 years for the Republic of Central America to collapse, at which point Costa Rica finally declared itself a fully independent country.

U.S. Citizen Illegally Attempts to Conquer Costa Rica

Once fully independent, Costa Rica finally began to blossom again. The Central Valley was discovered to be perfect for growing coffee, and this resulted in enough wealth to turn the country's capital, San José, into a modern city based on European standards.

In 1958, Costa Rica faced another external threat: a U.S. citizen by the name of William Walker. Walker was a filibuster, or person engaging in unauthorized warfare against a foreign country, and had already defeated neighboring Nicaragua in his designs to start a large slave-holding empire. But in his attempt to illegally conquer Costa Rica, Walker was famously defeated, with the catalyst of the battle becoming a legend. A local military drummer boy named Juan Santamaría set fire to Walker's stronghold, dying himself, but effectively ending the battle. Juan Santamaría is considered a national hero, and a national holiday, Juan Santamaría Day, is observed every April 11 to commemorate his noble death.

The Costa Rican Civil War

Costa Ricans settled back into a peaceful routine and grew coffee, bananas, and pineapples to export. Their peaceful way of life remained relatively uninterrupted until the Costa Rican Civil War in 1948 when they experienced a short but vicious struggle. José Figueres Ferrer, a U.S. educated engineer and self-described "farmer-socialist," led an armed uprising against a disputed presidential election, resulting in over 2,000 people killed over the course of only 44 days. It was a very bloody affair for the otherwise harmonious, tiny country, but resulted in Costa Rica's peaceful freedom once again. The aftermath of the war led to the election of Ferrer, and the creation of a new Costa Rican constitution guaranteeing universal suffrage. It also led to the disbanding of their military, making them one of the only nations in the world to do so (with incredible results that you'll read about in the Sustainability chapter). The country has since held 16 presidential elections in succession, all peaceful.

Costa Rica Today

In modern times, Costa Rica is a peaceful democracy that relies on technology and a vibrant trade in eco-tourism for its economy. Poverty has declined dramatically since the turn of the 21st century, though economic struggles still exist. In the past decade or so, Amazon (the world's largest e-commerce company), along with other global companies, has invested in making Costa Rica one of their providers of a wide range of corporate services. These Costa Rican businesses, in turn, employ local lawyers, accountants, software engineers, customer support, and more to provide these services. Providing these services worldwide has changed the economic playing field quite a bit.

Here is a snapshot of Costa Rica's top ten physical exports in 2019

Optical, technical, medical apparatus: US$3.7 billion (31.9% of total exports)

Fruits, nuts: $2.2 billion (18.9%)

Miscellaneous food preparations: $593.9 million (5.2%)

Electrical machinery, equipment: $471.6 million (4.1%)

Plastics, plastic articles: $378.9 million (3.3%)

Vegetable/fruit/nut preparations: $334.6 million (2.9%)

Pharmaceuticals: $325 million (2.8%)

Coffee, tea, spices: $285.6 million (2.5%)

Rubber, rubber articles: $270.3 million (2.4%)

Vegetables: $172.2 million (1.5%)

Today Costa Rica is considered a beacon of democratic light and environmental sustainability in Central America, the American continent, and all around the world.

The Language of Romance: 8 Tips on How to Sound Like a Local

The official language of Costa Rica is Spanish, spoken in a distinctive - yet very easy to understand - Costa Rican accent. Over 70% of people in Costa Rica speak Spanish as their first language and employ unique usages of certain Spanish words, just like we have slang in English (more on that later in this section). The second most popular language in Costa Rica is English, fluently spoken by an estimated 10.7% of the adult population. A much higher percentage of Costa Ricans can speak great conversational English, and an even larger percentage can speak a little bit of English, so don't worry!

On the Caribbean coast, locals with an African heritage often speak both Spanish and a language called Limonese Creole (also referred to as Criollo Limonense, Limonese, Limón Creole English, or Mekatelyu). "Mekatelyu" is actually a phrase of Limonese Creole, translating literally to "make I tell you," or in standard English, to "let me tell you." Limonese Creole is a dialect of Jamaican Creole, a creole language based on the English language. "Creole" is a unique language that develops over time from one or more distinctive languages (for example, in the U.S., Louisiana Creole is based on the French language, with influences from Spanish, African, and Native American roots). It is common in Costa Rica to refer to the Limonese people on the Caribbean coast by the French word "patois" (pronounced "patwah"); however, patois and creole are two very separate terms of reference to languages and dialects. Creole is a language that has developed over time from one or more languages; patois is a dialect, or regional differentiation, of a single language. An example of patois in the U.S. is the pidgin that is spoken by many native Hawaiians, along with English and Hawaiian.

Costa Rica is a nation rich in many indigenous languages spoken throughout the country, though these percentages are much lower, and you may be unlikely to encounter these languages on a casual Costa Rican holiday. However, it's always important and fun to learn about the country you are visiting, and a sign of respect to all of the inhabitants. And you never know where you might end up on a uniquely Costa Rican adventure! I haven't had the pleasure to practice any indigenous Costa Rican languages with a local yet, but I hope to one day.

There are five main indigenous languages spoken in Costa Rica, most of which are part of the Chibchan tribe's language family. Chibchan languages are a group of Indigenous South American languages that were spoken before AD 1500 (also known as CE 1500) in the area that now comprises Costa Rica, Nicaragua, Panama, Ecuador, and western Colombia. These languages include the more popular Bribrí, Cabécar, Maléku Jaíka, Buglere, and Guaymí, along with several other minority languages, each of which are described briefly below with their percentages (see APPENDIX A at the end of this book for a brief description of Costa Rica's indigenous languages and their percentages spoken in the country).

Speaking Spanish on Your Adventure: A Few Important Tips

To get the most out of your Costa Rican holiday, be sure to brush up on your Spanish skills before you arrive! It's always a safe bet to learn a few conversational words and phrases in the language of the country you're visiting and use them every chance you get. By making an effort to speak in the local language, you're showing respect to Costa Ricans as individuals and also to their culture.

By speaking some Spanish in Costa Rica, I've been invited to locals' homes for dinners, told about the best secret spots nearby, been given discounts, and was informed of the thriftiest ways to travel locally - information I probably would have never learned otherwise. If you learn some conversational Spanish, you are almost guaranteed to save lots of money. And the cherry on top of the cake is that you'll make a lot of amazing new friends. Plus, immersion is the best way to learn a new language. It's a win-win situation all around! Keeping that in mind, I'll cover a few common Spanish rules, words, and phrases, along with a few unique Costa Rican variations that will be fun to use with your new friends.

"Feminine," "Masculine," and "Neutral" Words

One of the most common features of the Spanish language is its use of neutral, masculine, and feminine nouns. This is because Spanish is a "Romance" language, or a language derived from Latin, the language spoken by the Roman Empire (other Romance languages include Portuguese,

French, Italian and Romanian).

This can make learning Spanish quite tricky (which you'll already know if you've ever tried to learn French). Luckily, if you are just learning conversational Spanish, there are only two simplified rules you need to remember for now:

> If you are referring to a male noun, add an "o" at the end. For example, a Costa Rican man is a Tico, and a male dog is a perro.

> If you are referring to a female noun, add an "a" at the end. For example, a Costa Rican woman is a Tica, and a female dog is a perra.

There are many other important feminine/masculine/neutral rules in Spanish that you need to know if you are serious about learning the language, but these are the two most important to remember for casual things like conversations, and the most important ones to show respect and avoid confusion.

"-ito" vs. "-ico" and Why Costa Ricans Refer to Themselves as "Ticos"

In standard Spanish, "-ito" is a suffix added to the end of words to show that something is small and/or cute. It's often used as a term of endearment, and also when talking to babies and small children. Here are a few examples: "perro" (dog) turns into "perrito" for a puppy, and baby Juana is called "Juanita."

However, in Costa Rican Spanish, the suffix "-ico" is used instead of the more common "-ito." Here are the same examples, Costa Rican style: "perro" (dog) turns into "perrico" for a puppy, and baby Juana is now called "Juanica."

Because of their uniquely peculiar twist on a standard Spanish suffix, Costa Ricans proudly refer to themselves as "Ticos." Pretty cute stuff, and it caught on - other nationalities refer to Costa Ricans as Ticos as well.

The Word for Towel is Not What You Think

The Spanish language is relatively uniform across all Latin-speaking countries, but there are always a few important differences in certain verbs and nouns... and some of them can be a little bit embarrassing to get wrong. In many Latin countries, "toalla" (pronounced "toh-aya") means "towel." In Costa Rica, "toalla" means tampon. To ask for a towel in Costa Rica, you should ask for a "paño" (pronounced "pan-yo").

"I'm Not Pregnant!" and other Spanish/English Cognates

Even if you don't know the Spanish word for something, you can try saying it in English, with a surprising amount of luck - there are many cognates (words that have both a similar sound and meaning) in both Spanish and English. For example, accident in Spanish = accidente, activities = actividades, adult = adulto, agent = agente, and so on. This can make learning Spanish very fun and funny, as you try out what you think might be the right pronunciation of an English/Spanish cognate.

Usually, this tactic works very well. Occasionally, you might cause some extreme confusion! For example, many people attempt a cognate when they want to say they are embarrassed and say, "Estoy embarazado" but this is a false cognate; "embarazado" means you are pregnant. You might want to try "Tengo vergüenza" (pronounced "ten-go ver-goo-enza") instead, which translates to "I am embarrassed." Don't worry about making mistakes when you are talking to local Costa Ricans, though - they are very kind, friendly people, and appreciate you making an effort to learn their language.

A Few Crucial Spanish Pronunciations

Spanish is considered to be one of the easiest languages to learn because it is a phonetic language or a language that has a direct correspondence between symbols and sounds. For example, the phrase "Gracias a Dios," which means "Thanks to God," is pronounced just like it's written. The majority of Spanish is phonetic.

Having said that, there are a few crucial pronunciations that you simply have to know if you are going to learn some conversational Spanish. Don't worry, it's not like French! There are only a few to remember. Here are the top three:

The Double L. In English, a double "ll" in a word doesn't change the sound of the letters; they are still the classic "L" sound. But in Spanish, a double "ll" in a word changes the sound to "y." For example, "llamar" ("to call") is pronounced "yamar" and "llave" ("key") is pronounced "yahveh."

The J Sound. In English, a "j" sounds like, well, a "j." In Spanish, a "j" always sounds like an "h." For example, "jamón" (ham) is pronounced "hamon," and "jungla" ("jungle") is pronounced "hungla."

The Silent H. In English, an "h" sometimes has a specific sound, and sometimes is silent. In Spanish, it is always a silent letter. For example, "huevo" ("egg") is pronounced "oo-ev-oh" and "hora" (hour) is pronounced "ora."

There are many other important pronunciations in Spanish if you are serious about learning the language, but these are the three most important to remember for casual things like conversations and reading menus.

As an extra bonus, here is an expert pronunciation tip that will make you sound like a natural Spanish speaker! When the letter "d" is in the middle of a word, for example, "comida" ("food"), you do not pronounce the classic "d" sound. Instead, you replace it with a "th" sound, similar to the hard "th" sound in the English word "thee" or "that" (not the "th" sound like in the word "with"). So, to sound like a local, you would pronounce it like this: "comitha."

Why Diacritics Might Save A Life

Diacritics are tiny marks or symbols written directly above or below a certain letter in a word to indicate a difference in pronunciation (as opposed to the same letter unmarked / with a normal pronunciation). A famous example of the importance of Spanish diacritics is this:

"Papá" with a diacritic mark, means "father." The emphasis is on the second syllable, so it is pronounced "PaPAH" instead of "papa."

"La papa" without a diacritic mark means "potato." There is no emphasis on any syllable.

That could make reading a menu (or hearing a local child talk to their father) very confusing if you don't know your diacritics! This particular diacritic is called an "acute accent" and signals where you need to put the emphasis on pronunciation in a word.

Of course, diacritics are important to know when you are learning to read or write Spanish. But there are many occasions when it behooves you to know a certain diacritic in spoken words, for example, the word "baño," which means "bathroom." This diacritic is often referred to as an "enya" because it changes the classic "n" sound to an "enya" sound. So instead of pronouncing "bahn-oh," what most people might assume phonetically reading the word "baño" with the "enya," it is correctly pronounced "bahn-yo." The enya diacritic turns the "n" sound into an "enya" sound. Another example is the word "Español" ("Spanish"). With the enya diacritic, this is correctly pronounced "Es-pan-yol" (not "Es-pan-ol").

There are several other Spanish diacritics, so be sure to do your research if you are planning on learning to read and write Spanish.

Speaking Spanish: Common Words & Phrases

No matter what country you're in, knowing how to say "please," "thank you," and "where is the bathroom" will make the quality of your life infinitely better (and that of those around you, too). To that end, here is a list of the most simple, common, important, and easy-to-remember Spanish words and phrases. You can easily memorize a few of these on the plane ride over!

Beer = Cerveza

Do you speak English? = ¿Hablas Inglés? (Inglés is another cognate!)

Doctor = Medica / Medico (another cognate!)

Food = Comida

Good morning = Buenos días

Good afternoon = Buenos tardes

Good night = Buenos noches

How much does it cost? = ¿Cuánto cuesta?

I don't speak Spanish = No hablo Español

I need = Yo necessito (another cognate!)

I want = Yo quiero (pronounced "yo kee-ero")

Nice to meet you = Mucho gusto

Now = Ahora (silent "h," so it is pronounced "a-ora")

Please = Por favor

Thank you = Gracias

Ticket = Boleto (airplane, train, bus)

Water = Agua (pronounced "ag-wah")

Where is the bathroom? = ¿Dónde está el baño?

You're welcome = De nada

Costa Rican "Pachuco" (Slang): Common Words and Phrases

Although Costa Ricans speak a relatively easy-to-understand version of Spanish, they do love their slang! Any conversation with a Tico or Tica is bound to be heavily peppered with Pachuco, or Costa Rican slang, so it's a great idea to learn the most common words and phrases (also called "Pachuquismos"). Plus, your new friends or the cashier at the supermarket will be very impressed when you whip out a Pachuquismo on them. I've had a lot of fun doing this, and it's often met with appreciative smiles and laughter. Here are just a few of the most commonly used Pachuco words and phrases, starting with the two phrases you will hear every single day in Costa Rica: Pura Vida and Mucho Gusto.

Pura Vida = Literally translates to "pure life," but similar to the word "Aloha" in Hawaiian, the phrase has various meanings. It can mean hello/goodbye/I am well/thank you/you're welcome/an adjective to describe a great person or thing, and much more. It is the most common thing said in Costa Rica by far, and considered by many to be the country's unofficial motto, generally meaning "we enjoy our beautiful life and are grateful for every day," more or less. This is a great peek into the Costa Rican mind.

Mucho gusto / Con gusto = with a lot of pleasure / with pleasure. This is used more commonly in Costa Rica to say "you're welcome" than the standard "de nada" normally used in Spanish-speaking countries. It can also mean "nice to meet you." It's another important peek into the Costa Rican personality - as a culture, they are very generous, giving, humble, and kind.

Acachete = That's cool / I feel good

Al chile = Really?!

Birra = Beer

Brete = Work

Buena nota = A good person

Despelote = A crazy mess!

Goma = Hangover

Harina = Money

Jumas = A drunk

Mae = Dude (pronounced "mai")

Manda huevo = C'mon!

Plata = Money

Por dicha = Thank goodness

Presa = Traffic

Que chiva = How great

Que lechero = How lucky

Que torta = What a mess!

Rojo = 1000 colones ("rojo" means red, the color of the bill)

Salado = Tough luck

Suave, suave = Give me a second, wait

Tuanis = Cool

Upe! = Used to get someone's attention, for example, knocking on someone's door

Zaguate = Street dog

Fun fact: some of the slang used in modern Costa Rica can be traced back to a strange kind of "code" that was invented by General Malespín, a political leader from El Salvador in the 1800s. The "code" swaps the letters b and t, a and e, i and o, f and g, and p and m. This is how the word "buenos" ("it's good") turned into "tuanis," and the word "trabajo" (work) turned into "breteji" or "brete" as it is commonly pronounced.

Best Time to Go: Costa Rica's Two Major Seasons and Why You Need to Know the Difference

As a tropical destination with a pleasantly temperate climate, Costa Rica is lovely to visit year-round. Warm weather and water make traveling here a joy to visitors no matter the season The air temperatures are fairly consistent year-round, never straying far from the 70F - 80F (21C - 27C) range found on the coastline. Higher altitudes enjoy a wider range of temperatures, with the "highlands" often 10F (7C) cooler than the coast with temperatures that can occasionally dip down as low as 50F (10C) in the highest altitudes. The sea in Costa Rica is pleasantly warm all year, ranging on average from 82F - 84F (28C - 29C).

Due to its proximity to the equator, this eco-friendly nation doesn't have a true "summer" or "winter" in the traditional sense. However, Costa Rica certainly has its own seasons, just like any place on Earth, and these seasons will affect the temperatures, rainfall, crowds, and prices of where you choose to travel. It's definitely worth checking out what the conditions will be like before you buy your ticket, no matter what type of tropical vacation you're planning. Below are brief but comprehensive descriptions of the different kinds of weather and seasons you will find in Costa Rica.

The "Dry" Season

A quick search online shows that Costa Rica's dry season, from December to April, is considered by most publications, travel companies, and travelers to be the best time to visit. This is because, during the dry season, it's sunny nearly every day: in other words, every day is a perfect beach day. If you can only travel during the public holidays, are limited on time (or unlimited in budget), and don't mind large crowds, then it's true - dry season is your best bet.

No matter which part of the dry season you book, you're practically guaranteed that every day will be rain-free and sunny. And for many who are looking to plan a vacation, that's all that matters. However, the guarantee of perfect weather comes with a price tag, so be prepared to pay "peak season" prices wherever you go. And make sure you book your travel and accommodation well in advance, as the holidays and the dry season, in general, tend to book out quickly and be much more crowded. To be safe, you should make your bookings for this season at least three months in advance.

Also, be prepared to be very hot! While the mercury doesn't necessarily skyrocket on the temperature gauge as it does in some tropical locations, the consistent heat and high humidity make for a reasonably hot day on most days. It's always wise to expect to perspire often while traveling in Costa Rica and drink a sufficient amount of water accordingly.

The most popular holidays in Costa Rica during the dry season are Christmas and New Year's, Easter weekend, and Spring Break (Spring Break is the traditional time for U.S. college and university students to travel abroad for a short vacation. Times vary each year, but it generally runs from late February to mid-April, with all of March being the peak period). It's absolutely crucial that you don't forget to factor in the Christmas holidays and Easter weekend - these are not only popular times for overseas tourists to travel, but more importantly, Costa Ricans love to celebrate these special holidays. Locals make a mass exodus from the towns and cities they live in and take their family and party vibes to the countryside and coastlines. Both of these holiday periods are a busy, happy, loud mass of parades, feasts, and celebrations seen all over the country (but mainly the coast). Will it be a fun time to travel? In the social sense, definitely, yes. Will it be extra crowded and much more expensive than normal everywhere? Absolutely, yes.

The dry season IS the most popular time to travel in Costa Rica. Nevertheless, the "wet" season, from May to November, is a wildly underappreciated gem for many tourists and visitors to this picturesque country.

The "Wet"/Green Season

Costa Rica is known for its beautifully lush, green landscapes and verdant rainforests; this is true year-round. However, there are some extra special treasures to be discovered during the wet season, and one of these is the way the whole country "blooms" during the rainy period. The emerald-green countryside, dense jungles, and rainforests are teeming with new life, blossoms, and green shoots. There is a fresh feeling in the air, almost of feasting after a famine - all of the local people, flora, and fauna are rejuvenated after the long, busy, dry season.

The wet season runs from May to November, with the peak rainy period generally occurring in the months of September and October, when the rain will often fall all day long. The increased rainfall increases the green, though it seems impossible, which is why the wet season is often referred to as the "green" season. Not only is the rich landscape thriving and thirstily drinking in all of the rainfall, but since this is considered off-season, you are far more likely to encounter excellent deals for accommodation, tours, transportation, and everything else you can imagine. Plus, the crowds are much smaller than in peak season, with some places and times experiencing a crowd so small as to be non-existent! Depending on what kind of traveler you are, this can be very enticing indeed. Even for those searching for social connectedness and fun parties will find it - the rains only serve to bring those who stuck around together, and the celebrations will only be more local and special for that reason.

The "green" season is also the best time of year for several of the more adventurous activities on offer in this diverse tropical landscape, such as surfing and whitewater rafting. Some of the largest (and depending on which surfer you ask, the best) ocean swells roll through this area in the rainy season. Many of the famous surf breaks are located near a river mouth where the waterway is flush with rain and pumping out into the ocean, which also affects the waves for surfing. Conversely, the rivers swollen with rainfall are perfect conditions for the adrenaline-fueled activity of whitewater rafting - with some of nature's finest scenery on display on either side of the river banks.

I mentioned earlier that it is important to choose your month wisely when traveling in Costa Rica in the dry season; this is even truer in the wet season. The significance of the different locations you choose to visit, and when, is crucial when booking for the wet season. The heaviest rainfall occurs in the northeast and southwest regions of the country, with several areas (such as the Osa Peninsula in the southwest) experiencing such a high rainfall in the peak of the wet season that some businesses and lodging options will temporarily close during this time. But don't worry, there are plenty of months and places during this time that are not all that rainy - for example, most of the Caribbean coast is fairly sunny and dry in comparison to the Pacific coast's rainy season.

Another thing to consider is the country's different celebrations during the green season. Although this period doesn't feature the show-stopping public holidays that the dry season does (such as Christmas and Easter weekend), there are still a few occasions to keep in mind. One of these is the little-known "veranillo" or "little summer" that can run anywhere from July to August. This time period brings less rain than the rest of the wet season, resulting in a brief respite of unusually dry, sunny weather. However, it's probably a good idea to avoid the first half of July, as this is the time when most school children go on a mid-term vacation with their families, and places will probably be very packed. Costa Ricans love their holidays!

It's true that you will have to plan and pack a little differently if you decide to travel to Costa Rica during their rainy season, but don't worry, we've got you covered - see our "What to Pack" chapter for a detailed list to pack for the wet season. If you choose to return to Costa Rica again, you may even find you prefer this time of year. Personally, I enjoyed it very much. For my first Costa Rican "wet season" experience, I found a little room to rent on a remote beach for a month. I set myself up to surf every morning, write every afternoon, and surf every sunset. I couldn't have been happier. I found the lull of gently swooshing, or at times heavily pounding, rain for intervals throughout each day to be very conducive to my workflow. I loved the reduced crowds. There were long periods of sunshine, still, and a sense of refreshment in the community and surrounding nature. Everything was getting revived, and I could feel it. Here is one of my favorite memories of that time:

"At sunset, I stopped typing, put my laptop away, and grabbed my surfboard. There were some beautiful waves to catch that afternoon. But the very best thing about the day was the rain. It sprinkled lightly for a few minutes, a little foreplay before it really started pouring. Then the rain magically transformed the seascape into one of the prettiest things I've ever seen. Every fat raindrop was a jewel on the water, so the water was covered with jewels. The softly strong swish of the rain joined up with the crash of the waves to make special music. The waves became endless undulating mountains in the distance, partially obscured by mist, like real mountains in the distance. Everything was a shade of gray in a diffused light, and words are not even sufficient to describe it. It was so incredibly beautiful!"

So, you see? There are different types of beauty to behold in every Costa Rican season.

Weather Varies Between the Pacific & Caribbean Coasts

The weather patterns on the Pacific and Caribbean coasts vary widely, and throughout the year, there are several differences worth noting. During the heaviest rainfall on the Pacific coast in September and October, it is often relatively dry and sunny on the Caribbean coast. Similarly, when the Caribbean coast is experiencing part of its rainy season (from November through January in the north Caribbean, and from April through August in the south Caribbean), it may be drier on the Pacific coast. For this reason, it's always a wise idea to check the specific weather patterns of the areas you will be visiting.

Two of the main causes of these marked differences in weather patterns on either coast are the stunning Tilaran and Cordillera mountain ranges. Together, the mountains form the Continental Divide that effectively splits the country into two distinctive sides, and the presence of these immense mountain ranges often diffuses a storm before it can reach the other side of the country.

Very occasionally, there is a weather condition in the northeast of the country where there is a southward penetration of cold air masses that have developed in the continental United States; however, this happens very rarely. There is also a variance in rainfall each year depending on the status of the El Niño–Southern Oscillation, so it may be worth your time to double-check on this year's weather patterns as well before you make your plans for the dry or wet season.

The Rainforests Are a World of Their Own

An important thing to keep in mind when planning your travel to Costa Rica is that all of the rainforests, while generally more "dry" between December through April, never have a true "dry" season. Precipitation is fairly consistent year-round, and even when it's not raining, heavy mists can come and go, so it's wise to be prepared no matter what time of year you choose to visit. Don't fret about getting a little bit wet - it's all part of the exciting adventure that is Costa Rica. It's always a great idea to pack an extra dry set of socks and a rain jacket, though. Be sure to check out the "What to Pack" chapter before planning what to bring on your trip.

The "Shoulder" Season

If you're having a hard time deciding on which time of year

to visit this wonderful country, first, put your worries aside. No matter what time you choose to come, there are uniquely wonderful adventures to experience, and new beauties to discover. Having said that, if you just can't choose between the more affordable and less crowded wet season or the more expensive but sunny dry season - try the "shoulder" season! May and November are often referred to as the "shoulder" season, as they fall smack dab in the middle of peak season and rainy season, and offer a bit more flexibility in different budgets and more options with activities. Due to the fickle nature of weather patterns around the world, it's impossible to guarantee that your trip in May will be perfectly "dry" or that your vacation in November will be "only a little wet"; however, it's a pretty darn good bet that you will get the best of both worlds, and you really can't lose either way! Just be prepared with appropriate rainy weather gear if you decide the shoulder season is right for you.

Adventures by the Ocean: Activities & Sightseeing

If you love the great outdoors, you will never run out of things to do and see in this treasure trove of a country. Here is just a shortlist of how you can have fun in Costa Rica, and it is by no means conclusive: nature walks, yoga, swimming, surfing, learning Spanish, fishing, SUP, whale watching, freediving, snorkeling, beach walks, hiking... and guess what? These activities are all free if you choose to do them on your own or with a friend. There are many secrets and hidden gems in Costa Rica - if you know where to look and when.

If you want to invest in a special class or a guided tour, your options are even more diverse, as you can do any of the activities mentioned above along with ATV tours, horseback riding, staying with a local family, canyoning, safaris, ziplining through a rainforest, sunset sailing, deep-sea fishing, and so much more. Even if your style leans more towards sipping a craft cocktail on a chaise lounge next to a sparkling pool, we've got you covered. This is hardly an exhaustive list of the activities you can find in this epic country, but consider it a summary of some of the best highlights.

Many of the activities listed below can be done for free and/or by yourself if you choose - with a few exceptions. When snorkeling and surfing, you should always have a snorkel/surf buddy to be safe (especially in a new location), and if you don't bring your own gear, you will have to rent it. If you decide to dive deep into the enchanting underworld of Costa Rica's oceans, you must rent your equipment, and for nearly every dive site, you will have to shell out a few bucks for a guided tour or boat ride - so worth it for an unforgettable memory, though. And finally, you may not be familiar with some of the activities listed below, in which case, you can always take a class or tour and make some new friends along the way!

Below, I've listed some of the best beaches in the country, the top scuba diving sites, the best surf spots, and everything you need to know about whale watching. Read on to discover your future adventures in the magical land of Costa Rica.

Get ready - it's a long list of (mostly) FREE & budget fun!

Beautiful Beaches of Costa Rica: 17 of My Favorites to Get You Started

If you like piña coladas, getting caught in the rain, and long walks on the beach, this is definitely the country for you! Both the Pacific and Caribbean shores share a multitude of diversity on their coastlines, so you will always have something new and exciting to discover no matter where you are. Some beaches are popular and crowded with happy beachgoers, and others are long stretches of wild, peaceful shorelines with not another soul in sight. Here are just a few of our favorites for snorkeling, freediving, shell-collecting, and just heading out for a stroll on the lovely playa ("playa" means "beach" in Spanish). Fun fact: all beaches in Costa Rica, right up to where the sand ends, are public property.

Popular Costa Rican Beaches

These locations are close to people, restaurants, and accommodations.

1. **Cocles.** Playa Cocles is a picturesque little beach, situated between the famous port city of Puerto Viejo to the north and the sleepy little town of Cahuita to the south. It has soft, tan sand and clear blue waters, and because it's so accessible and close to Puerto Viejo, it's often a little bit crowded on a beautiful day (so, pretty much every day).

2. **Conchal**. Playa Conchal is perhaps the most famous beach in Costa Rica, known and loved for its feature attraction: a beach that is composed of gazillions of crushed up little shells. Isn't that what sand is made up of in general, you say? Well, yes, but not like here! This is sand-in-the-making. You have to see it to understand how special it is.

Plus, post-walk swimming is fantastic.

3. **Espadilla**. Playa Espadilla is located right in front of the little seaside village of Manuel Antonio and the entrance to the much-loved Manuel Antonio Park (more on that in the next section!). The long, sandy beach stretches for over a mile and is frequented often by travelers and fun-loving families.

4. **Jacó**. Playa Jacó is an extension of the busy town of Jacó: both full of fun-loving travelers and lots of surfers. On a big swell day, it's fun to walk along the gray sand beach and watch surfers show off their best moves! And at sunset or sunrise, you'll be treated to one of Jacó's famous sunsets.

5. **Guiones**. Playa Guiones is a well-known beach; however, it falls somewhere in between "popular" and "peaceful" on the spectrum. It features almost a three-mile-long stretch of sparkling white sand, along with a multitude of good vibes, hippies, ex-pats, and talented surfers.

6. **Sámara**. Playa Sámara is a horseshoe-shaped gem of a beach with consistently calm waters, thanks to a small island protecting the bay. It's a long beach, which makes this popular destination a little more peaceful since there's room for everyone.

7. **Santa Teresa**. Playa Santa Teresa is probably one of the "coolest" beaches in Costa Rica with the younger generations - everywhere you look, there are travelers, ex-pats, backpackers, surfers, and locals enjoying the long, pristine beach bordered by the charming village of Santa Teresa and the dense jungle behind it. Though it can get crowded, it still has that end-of-the-world feeling, and the tide pools at the far south end are gorgeous. Just be warned if you wear contact lenses and plan on visiting in the dry season - it can get very dusty in town, from the constantly churning dirt road. I had to wear my eyeglasses while walking around town.

8. **Tamarindo**. Playa Tamarindo is one of the most popular beaches in all of Costa Rica, and for good reason: it's a big favorite with fun-loving backpackers and tourists, and has a thriving nightlife. The beach isn't that long, but it's a great walk for people-watching, shell-collecting, watching surfers, and is known for its fiery sunsets. I've seen some of the most stunning sunsets of my life here!

Peaceful Costa Rican Beaches

These locations are off the beaten track, further from civilization. They are a great place to get a little "lost" in, if that's more your style.

1. **Biensanz**. Playa Biensanz is a treasure that you have to discover by walking down a ten-minute hiking trail through the jungle. And it's so worth it! Tranquility and wildlife abound.

2. **Carate**. Playa Carate is a wild, black sand beach right next door to the Corcovado National Park. If deserted jungle beaches and abundant wildlife are what you're after, this is the beach for you.

3. **Chiquita**. Playa Chiquita is a lovely, secluded white sand beach with crystal blue waters bordered by multiple natural bays and the sleepy little village of Chiquita, south of Puerto Viejo on the Caribbean side.

4. **Dominical**. Playa Dominical is a pleasant change in scenery after a long bus ride, with dark rocky sand and deep blue water bordered by wild jungle. With some of the most consistent surf to watch year-round, gorgeous sunsets, and dolphins never far away, it's a win-win. There are also several stunning waterfalls nearby.

5. **Malpaís**. Playa Malpaís is a beautiful, almost mysterious slice of heaven. Discover the magic in rocky tide pools and long stretches of soft sand.

6. **Manzanillo**. Playa Manzanillo is located within a natural refuge, making this nearly 5-mile long beach (broken up by rocky cliffs creating perfectly protected swimming coves) the perfect spot to see wildlife and experience heavenly exotic seclusion.

7. **Ostional**. Playa Ostional is a protected beach and one of the major nesting sites for Ridley sea turtles. With its dark sand, crystal clear water, and teeming wildlife, it's a perfect beach walk - just be sure to check it's not turtle nesting

season (July to December) - when you will have to book a tour to walk on the beach.

8. **Punta Uva**. Playa Punta Uva is less than four miles (about 6km) south of busy Puerto Viejo on the Caribbean side, but you'd never know it. Quiet, white sand beaches are flanked by turquoise waters, and a palm-tree dotted shoreline.

9. **San Juanillo**. Playa San Juanillo is sometimes referred to as "the most beautiful beach in Costa Rica." It's two white-sand beaches meet in a rocky point with an especially spectacular view, and the clear waters are essentially all yours - the only civilization nearby is the tiny little local village of San Juanillo.

10. **Uvita**. Playa Uvita is last on our list, but certainly not least. In between long stretches of wild, lovely beaches is a unique geographical landmark in the shape of a whale's tail! You can learn more about this special location in our "Whale Watching in Costa Rica" section.

Dive Deep into Costa Rica's Enchanting Underworld: 8 of the Best Scuba Sites on Earth

Scuba diving in the pristine azure waters of Costa Rica's oceans is on many a bucket list, and for good reason. The healthy, largely protected waters of both the Caribbean and the Pacific are teeming with a rich diversity of sea life: schools of exotic fish, manta rays, many kinds of sea turtles, dolphins, sharks, nudibranchs (strange, beautiful little sea creatures - if you've never heard of them, look them up!), and an incredible landscape of reef topography, not to mention a nine-month-long whale season.

Did you know that the Pacific ocean is the world's oldest and largest ocean, covering over 51% of the planet? 75% of all saltwater fish species live in the waters of the Pacific, and Costa Rica is blessed with warm weather year-round, making this one of the best places on Earth to scuba dive!

Many of the popular dive spots in Costa Rica require a boat ride and/or a guide. This is because most of the best diving spots in the country are in hard-to-reach places, and some of them are also located in a natural or wildlife sanctuary or refuge that is protected by law from too much human traffic. Plus, because of Costa Rica's international scuba standards, it's guaranteed that your diving guide or divemaster will be incredibly knowledgeable about the history, location, and wildlife of your dive, and maybe even point out a few secrets to you along the way. Worth it! There are many friendly local businesses that will take you on any guided tour of Costa Rica's underwater world that you can dream up, so you won't ever have to worry about options. Here are a few of the favorite scuba spots in Costa Rica.

1. **Gandoca Manzanillo Wildlife Refuge, Southern Caribbean Coast.** This refuge is one of the best spots for diving on the Caribbean Coast, with Punta Uva and Manzanillo scuba dive sites. There are lovely coral reefs, little bays, inlets, and tiny islands nearby, along with manatees, dolphins, crocodiles, eels, rays, blacktip sharks, and dolphins, to name a few! Depths up to 60 feet (18m).

2. Isla del Coco or "Cocos Island," Puntarenas Province. Described by Jacques Cousteau as "the most beautiful island in the world," Isla Del Coco has many claims to fame. It was the location for the opening scenes of the original Jurassic Park, is a UNESCO World Heritage Site, and is considered to be the best spot in all of Costa Rica for scuba diving. Because the island is located 375 miles (603km) from shore, divers can only experience Cocos Island by chartering a private "live-aboard" boat - no overnight visitors are allowed on the island, which is a nature reserve. So, it's not exactly a budget activity, but I'm listing it anyway because it's a world treasure.

Suitable only for experienced divers, you can expect to be delighted by some of the world's largest schools of hammerhead sharks, along with manta rays, eagle rays, dolphins, whales, tiger sharks, Galapagos sharks, white tip sharks, maybe even whale sharks and orcas on a very lucky day, sea lions, sea turtles, and even a rare scalloped hammerhead shark. The landscapes don't fade into the background, either - Cocos Island boasts underwater caves, over 30 species of coral, volcanic tunnels, and crystal clear azure waters. The visibility can vary due to the plankton-rich waters around the island, which are also responsible for the diversity of sea life. Depths reach up to 131 feet (40m).

3. **Cahuita National Park, Southern Caribbean Coast**.

This quiet park is known for being one of the largest living coral reefs of Costa Rica, featuring over 35 different species of living coral, along with many magical seahorses and other tropical fish. Don't underestimate it! Plus, on land, the park has a nature trail that follows the shoreline for almost six miles. Visibility is highly dependent on rainfall; heavy rains can make the water murky. Depths are generally shallow at around 15 feet.

4. **Caño Island Biological Reserve, Osa Peninsula**.

There are many amazing locations for scuba diving around the entire Osa Peninsula that are suitable for novices, intermediate, and pros. But the most famous one is the Caño Island Biological Reserve. Because it is protected as a reserve, there are a few rules to follow: for example, you can only dive at specifically designated diving spots around the reserve, and only ten divers are allowed in the water per dive. But this is great news for everyone! It means that the crystal clear waters are uncrowded by humans, allowing for the best view of sea life.

Depending on the day, you may see giant manta rays (there have been reports of up to 20 foot/6m wingspans), the jumping Mobula ray, white tip sharks, bull sharks, nurse sharks, spotted dolphins, pufferfish, sea turtles, dozens of schools of tropical fish, barracuda, octopus, gorgeous underwater landscapes, a million shades of coral, humpback and pilot whales, and if you're really, really lucky, you might catch a glimpse of the elusive whale shark with its beautiful spotted pattern. An important thing to remember is that the weather varies widely on the Osa Peninsula, receiving a lot of rainfall at certain times of the year, which affects visibility.

Each of the Caño Island Biological Reserve diving locations has its own charm and unique features - be sure to read up on them before heading out! Here are the designated scuba spot names and their depths:

Bajo del Diablo (or "Devil's Rock"). Depth: 20 - 150 ft (6 - 45m)

Bajo del Diablo Deep. Depth: 6 - 115 ft (20 - 35m)

Cueva del Tiburon (or "Shark Cave"). Depth: 33 - 55 ft (10 - 15m)

The Coral Gardens. Depth: 13 - 40 ft (5 - 12m)

Paraíso (or "Paradise"). Depth: 60 to 72 ft (18 - 22m)

Marenco Rock. Depth: 50 to 60 feet (15 - 18m)

Barco Hundido (or "Shipwreck" - no ship here, though!). Depth: 15-20 meters (50-70 feet)

Los Arcos (or "Arches"). Depth: 33 - 55 ft (10 - 17m)

El Faro (or "Lighthouse" - no lighthouse here anymore, though!). Depth: 66 - 82 ft (20 - 25m)

5. **Catalina Islands, Guanacaste**. The beautiful Catalina Islands are home to a smorgasbord of sea life, including eagle rays, moray eels, white tip sharks, sea turtles, octopus, seahorses, and so much more, making it a top dive spot for many scuba enthusiasts. The visibility is generally great year-round, in all seasons. Diving depths vary from 18 to 75 feet (6 to 23m).

6. **Gulf of Papagayo, Guanacaste**. The Gulf of the Papagayo Peninsula offers dozens of diverse dive spots, all just a twenty-minute boat ride or less away from the nearby town of Playas del Coco. With its calm, protected bays and inlets, sunken boat, low-lying volcanic islands, meandering channels, rich reef life, schools of fish so thick that they "block out the sun," you won't want to miss this diving treasure of an area. The temperatures and visibility here range widely throughout the year, depending on the weather and season, so be sure to do your homework. Diving depths

range from 15 feet to 100 feet.

7. **Gulfo Dulce, Osa Peninsula**. The Gulfo Dulce on the Osa Peninsula has unique marine and terrestrial ecosystems making it the perfect destination for those who love wildlife on both land and sea. This area is home to an enormous population of spinner dolphins, so you might catch a surprise acrobatic performance during your adventure! The spinner dolphins sometimes join up in super-pods (when over 1,000 dolphins gather together, also known as "mega-pods"... yes, this really happens!) and are an incredible wonder to watch, whether from the boat or in the water.

8. **Islas Murciélagos ("Bat Islands"), Guanacaste Province.** Located right at the tip of the

Santa Rosa National Park, the Bat Islands are one of the more popular spots for experienced divers and adrenaline junkies. Adrenaline junkies, you say? Yes! One of the main draws here is the very active, healthy population of bull sharks - that will get anyone's heart pounding! Divers can also expect to enjoy seeing various species of rays, sea turtles, whales, dolphins, and other sharks.

The Surfer's Secret Handbook:17 Dream Collections of Waves

Many a surfer from around the world has gazed lovingly at photos and videos on the internet, read stories in various books and magazines, and just generally drooled from afar at the perfection of Costa Rican surf culture. This is because Costa Rica's surf breaks are counted among some of the best in the world!

If you are an experienced surfer AND an adrenaline junkie, you can try your luck in the jaws of Salsa Brava on the Caribbean side, or Playa Grande and Pavones on the Pacific coast. If you're a beginner looking for your perfect first surfing destination, you can't go wrong with lovely Nosara, Sámara, or Tamarindo, and their many friendly surf schools. If you're somewhere in between beginner and expert, there are a multitude of options to satisfy every single surfer soul. Whether you venture to the Caribbean vibes, national parks, and remote beauty of the east coast, or follow the well-traveled route of the Pacific coast that offers a more diverse range of options including surf breaks, restaurants, and accommodation, you are guaranteed to have the time of your life. Here's a list of the best surf breaks in Costa Rica.

1. **Boca Barranca**. Considered to be the second-longest left-hand wave in Costa Rica (Pavones is first), this break offers an irresistible variety of dreamy conditions for many longboarders (and bodyboarders, too). Though the pollution in the water here can occasionally reach unpleasant levels, especially after a rain, the point break provides such a long and satisfying ride that it can draw crowds regardless of water clarity. Just take a shower afterward, and enjoy the ride!

Location: Boca Barranca, Puntarenas

Level: Intermediate

Type of Break: River mouth/reef and sand

2. **Dominical**. This is a fast and hollow wave that breaks on the beach of a very tiny, very chill village, and also breaks in front of the river mouth nearby. Barrels abound here! But be warned: it's a heavy, fast break, and many a surfer and board have been injured here without exercising the proper amount of caution.

Location: Dominical, Puntarenas

Level: Intermediate, Advanced

Type of Break: Beach/sand

3. **Jacó**. One of Costa Rica's beloved specialties - a surf break that offers consistent, excellent surf for every level, depending on the swell and the day. Surf schools abound, and a shuttle regularly heads south to Playa Hermosa 10 minutes south for more advanced surfers on good swell days. The very popular Jacó break has left and right-hand waves to satisfy every surfer and can hold its own admirably when larger swells roll in.

Location: Jacó, Puntarenas

Level: Beginner, Intermediate, Advanced

Type of Break: Beach/sand

4. **Langosta**. This break features at least five different waves you can surf, depending on the day and swell, which is, of course, extra fun! The sections of this break cover it all: reef, beach, and river mouth. Thanks to all of the options, there are left hand and right hand breaking waves, and it's conveniently located just one mile south of the bustling, happy town of Tamarindo. Take care with the rocky shallows and shifting sandbars, and you will enjoy A-frame waves, barrels, walls, carving, and more.

Location: Tamarindo, Guanacaste

Level: Intermediate, Advanced

Type of break: Reef, beach, river mouth / rocky, reef, sandy

5. **Malpaís**. Like many things in life, if it's harder to get to, it's more fun! Malpaís might be tricky to get to, but as a diversified break that features not only consistent waves for different level surfers but also a gorgeous stretch of isolated coastline, it's most definitely worth it. Especially if you are a "goofy foot" surfer or a surfer that prefers left-handed waves. You can choose from either an advanced-surfers-only reef break with barrels (Sunset Reef) or a more sheltered point

break called Mar Azul. Beware the razor-sharp shallow reef of the former and the rocky bottom of the latter.

Location: Cóbano, Nicoya Peninsula, Puntarenas

Level: Intermediate, Advanced

Type of Break: Reef, beach/reef, and sand

6. **Manzanillo**. One of the more remote beaches on the Nicoya Peninsula, Manzanillo, really only works well with bigger swell from the west and northwest. But when it works, it works! It features right and left-hand waves that break over a rocky offshore reef, and you can often expect powerful, hollow tubes.

Location: Manzanillo, Nicoya Peninsula, Puntarenas

Level: Intermediate, Advanced

Type of Break: Beach break/sand and reef

7. **Nosara**. Nosara is considered by many to be "the perfect place to surf," and you'll quickly see why - this laidback beachy town has consistent beginner waves year-round and charm to spare. You won't lack for friendly surf school options, the atmosphere is welcoming, and if you are an

intermediate or advanced surfer, don't doubt there is plenty for you to enjoy as well. It just depends on the swell. There are several breaks here (Guiones, Ostional, Marbella) offering something for everyone on this happy long stretch of stunning coastline.

Location: Nosara, Nicoya Peninsula, Guanacaste

Level: Beginner, Intermediate, Advanced

Type of Break: Beach, reef/sand, reef, and rocky

8. **Pavones**. Oh, Pavones. Remember when we mentioned how much fun it is to find your way to a hard-to-get-location? Well, surfers set on experiencing one of the world's longest left-hand waves can eat their heart out in this tiny, isolated town! Located right at the bottom of the country near Panama, this surf break is a little slice of heaven for experienced surfers. This three-section wave can get very crowded, especially when larger swells roll in. You have to work hard for this very worthy treasure: get ready for one of the longest bus trips of your life, along with some long paddling sessions thanks to the strong rips on either side of the river mouth.

Location: Pavones, Puntarenas

Level: Intermediate, Advanced

Type of Break: Point, river mouth/mostly rocky, some sand

9. **Playa Avellanas**. Another absolutely lovely, remote surf spot offering a variety of waves for every surfer to enjoy. Just about five miles / ten kilometers south of busy Tamarindo, this location handles large swells exceptionally well, has right and left-hand waves, and offers five different wave peaks: La Purruja, Lola's, Palo Seco, River Mouth, and Little Hawai'i. Depending on the day, a surfer of any level experience will find a wave for them in this isolated, gorgeous stretch of coastline.

Location: Tamarindo, Guanacaste

Level: Beginner, Intermediate, Advanced

Type of Break: Reef, beach/reef, and sand

10. **Playa Grande**. Just a hop, skip, and a jump away from nearby Tamarindo town (well, a little walk or bike ride and very short boat ride across the river), this is an absolutely beautiful wave when it's working. Playa Grande is a consistent, quality beach break that works best in a south swell and offers a variety of fun: A-frame, tube rides, lefts, and rights. Be warned: DO NOT cross the river by swimming in an attempt to save a dollar - there have been crocodile attacks to the careless individual, and this rule is true for any river in Costa Rica. Don't cross any river without asking a local first. This surf break is worth a little trip. While it can get crowded, you won't regret it!

Location: Tamarindo, Guanacaste

Level: Beginner, Intermediate

Type of Break: Beach/sand

11. **Playa Hermosa**. Hermosa is the more exclusive, expensive (if you're looking at accommodation and

restaurants), and very fun twin of Playa Jacó. If you're traveling on a budget, it's wiser to just get a shuttle or bus from Jacó every day instead of staying here. It's just about five miles or ten kilometers south of Jacó town and has been called heaven by many an intermediate or advanced surfer. Large swells offer barrels, punchy lips, and adrenaline-fueled waves for the experienced.

Location: Jacó, Puntarenas

Level: Intermediate, Advanced

Type of Break: Beach/sand

12. **Playa Negra**. Playa Negra has a bit of a claim to world-class fame as one of the breaks featured in the sequel to the famous old surf film, "The Endless Summer." With a left-hand, consistently fast wave offering barrels, this wave is popular with many a surfer seeking that warm-water adrenaline rush. The location is a bit isolated, but you can stay with local families just a short bike ride away, or in the nearby village of Cahuita.

Location: Los Pargos, Guanacaste

Level: Intermediate/Advanced

Type of Break: Reef/reef and sand

13. **Salsa Brava**. A little addition to your conversational Spanish and knowledge of Costa Rican surf culture: "Salsa Brava" translates to "Angry Sauce," a perfect title for this very heavy, fast, and hollow break reminiscent of the kind of barrels you'd find in Hawai'i. Large swells from the east and strong winds from the south combine to make one of the most epic and powerful waves in Costa Rica. Don't attempt to enjoy these fast right-hand barrels unless you are a very experienced surfer looking for an adrenaline rush, and if you are, then enjoy the unique thrills of this world-class wave!

Location: Puerto Viejo, Limón

Level: Intermediate, Advanced

Type of Break: Reef/reef

14. **Sámara**. This fun, quirky little town has a vibrant nightlife - and daylife - that many travelers will never forget. And there's a little bit of surf for everyone, depending on the swell (as long as you're not a diehard tube rider or big wave chaser). Lovely little surf schools abound in a protected bay perfect for learning how to ride your first waves, and Sámara break is conveniently located right in front of the town. For the more advanced, there is nearby Buena Vista break (a 5min drive or 30min walk away), plus as a bonus, when the swell hits just right, almost any surfer will enjoy the Nosara break, too.

Location: Sámara, Guanacaste

Level: Beginner, Intermediate

Type of Break: Beach/sand

15. **Santa Teresa**. Many a surfer's dreams have come true in this remote, lively town on the Nicoya Peninsula. It might take a little longer to get here than other, easy-access breaks, but it's worth it! There are many sections of surf peaks along this very beautiful section of coastline, featuring consistent waves, hollow waves, heavy waves - all depends on the day,

but you're almost guaranteed to have something every day. With the multiple peaks, it doesn't always get too crowded but beware of the very strong rip current and rocky sections in places.

Location: Cóbano, Nicoya Peninsula, Puntarenas

Level: Intermediate/Advanced

Type of Break: Beach/sand, some reef

16. **Tamarindo**. Tamarindo is perhaps one of the most famous towns of Costa Rica for many reasons, including a vibrant nightlife, oodles of happy backpackers from everywhere on Earth, and for being one of the best places to

learn how to surf. With the consistent swell, long beach, sandy bottom, and multiple peaks, it's hard to be disappointed here. There are many surf schools and friendly faces, and some of the best sunsets around. It's not just for beginners, though. There are lefts, rights, and some very fun waves with bigger swells. It can get crowded, but it's still one of the best breaks in Costa Rica, and there's always Playa Langosta to the south or Playa Grande to the north (both offering a bit more variety for the experienced surfers).

Location: Tamarindo, Guanacaste

Level: Beginner, Intermediate

Type of Break: Beach/sand

17. **Witches' Rock / Playa Naranjo**. Because of their location in a natural sanctuary, Witch's Rock and Playa Naranjo (don't get this name confused with the town called Playa Naranjo, which is somewhere else) rarely gets crowded. Witch's Rock break is so named because it breaks right in front of a giant volcanic rock formation that was allegedly cursed by a witch. As a wave offering A-frames, lefts, rights in large and intense outside sets, Witches' Rock is not for the faint of heart. Playa Naranjo itself offers some very fun inside sets as well. Because of their remote location,

there is no accommodation or town close by, and for this reason, many just opt to catch a boat here for a few hours of wild fun.

Location: Santa Rosa National Park, Guanacaste

Level: Intermediate/Advanced

Type of Break: Beach/sand

The Thrilling, Magical Experience of Whale Watching in Costa Rica

It's almost impossible to have a bad day when mammals the

size of buses are frolicking happily in the sparkling waters nearby. This tiny Central American country has the unique and amazing title of having more humpback whales in residence in their waters for longer than anywhere else on Earth. Quite the claim! These gentle aquatic giants approach Costa Rica at different times of the year as they migrate from the northwest (Alaska and California), the south (the Antarctic), and the northeast (North Atlantic) for a total combined humpbacks-in-residence time of approximately nine months.

Let's take a closer look at the different types of whales in Costa Rica (there are many), the best time of year to see them, the best places to see them, and a few fun facts about these beautiful creatures.

The warm, safe waters of Costa Rica draw many different types of whales from all over the world, but as far as whale-watching goes, humpback whales are the king. This is because these whales are very playful and spend much of their time in the area relatively close to shore - close enough to be very visible to the human eye from land or from a boat. The other types of whales that live, visit, or frequent the waters around Costa Rica spend most of their time in deeper water and, as such, are rarer to see.

Humpback Whales

The humpback is considered to be many people's "favorite whale" not only because it is the most visible whale to humans, but also because it is so active on the surface of the water. Humpback antics have overjoyed many a whale watcher, as the huge mammals actually launch their giant bodies out of the water, slap their dorsal fin loudly on the surface repeatedly, and much more. Be sure to have your camera ready for these incredible moments that you will never forget! I've watched humpback whales for years, and have never tired of it, and never lost the thrill. Not even close. They are a truly incredible sight to behold.

The humpback whale is a species of baleen whale. They are named "baleen" for the way they feed, which is beautiful in its simplicity. Baleen are the whale's "teeth," except that they are not normal teeth; in fact, they are made of keratin, the same thing human hair and fingernails are made out of. They are very long and thin, similar to bristles. Now imagine the whale opening its mouth wide and sucking in a huge mouthful of water, and then closing its mouth and pushing the water out through its baleen or "teeth" - like a giant strainer. This allows krill and other small animals to be trapped inside the whale's mouth and then be swallowed as a food source. Fun, right?

Humpback whales are categorically divided by naming them from the area where they originated. In Costa Rica, there are three types of humpback whales: Alaska/California or "Northern Humpback" whales, Antarctic or "Southern Humpback" whales, and "North Atlantic Humpback" St. Lawrence whales. The humpback whale is named for the distinctive hump on its back. Its scientific name, Megaptera novaeangliae, means "big-winged" and describes its long, beautiful pectoral fins.

The other whales in residence or visiting the warm waters of Costa Rica, which perhaps you may see one day if you are incredibly lucky (but it's very rare), are pilot whales, blue whales, and pseudo-orca whales. You might be asking yourself, what about the whale sharks mentioned in the scuba diving section? Whale sharks are actually just a (beautiful) type of gigantic, slow-moving shark, in addition to being the largest known fish species in existence (yes, sharks are a type of fish).

Blue Whales

The blue whale has a very big claim to fame it's the largest living animal on our planet! These breathtakingly large mammals can weigh up to 200 tons, which is approximately the weight of thirty-three elephants, if you can imagine that, and can measure up to 80 to 100 feet (24 to 30 meters). One of the most famous examples of their gargantuan proportions is that their heart alone is the size of a Volkswagen Beetle. Perhaps a lesser-known fact about blue whales is that they are also the loudest animal on Earth - their calls and low-frequency whistles can be heard for hundreds of miles and reach up to 188 decibels. For reference, a screaming jet engine taking off reaches 140 decibels. These gentle giants can live up to eighty or ninety years in the wild.

Pseudo-orca Whales

Pseudo-orca whales (also known as false killer whales, false pilot whales, or blackfish) are actually not whales at all. They are so named because their skull and coloring can often imitate other mammals in the dolphin family. They are actually a type of (very large) oceanic dolphin. Males can grow up to around 20 feet (6m) and weigh up to 3,000 pounds. Pseudo-orca whales are highly social and very playful animals, and they have even been known to offer their food to humans diving and snorkeling nearby.

Pilot Whales

Pilot whales, like pseudo-orca whales, are actually a member of the dolphin family, and, fun fact - they are second only to the killer whale (which is also a type of dolphin, hilariously) in size in the dolphin family. Adult males grow up to 20 feet (6.1 m) in length and up to 3 tons in weight. Adult females grow up to 16 feet (4.9 m) and up to 1.5 tons in weight. Pilot whales are well-known for their incredible intelligence, considered equal to that of their more famous cousin, the bottlenose dolphin.

Best Time of Year to See Whales in Costa Rica

Because Costa Rica is in such a unique location, the country, its inhabitants, and its visitors get to enjoy the rare joy of humpback whales approaching from three different directions, spread out over different times of the year. You have a pretty good chance of seeing a humpback whale in Costa Rica for an incredible nine months out of the year! Not every month is created equal in whale-watching, though. There are some months where you're practically guaranteed to see humpbacks frolicking off the coastline and other months where you may have to search high and low to find one of the friendly ocean behemoths in the distance. It also depends on which coast you will be visiting.

Whale watching from December to April (when

Northern Humpback whales migrate south from Alaska/California). After feeding on krill (very tiny, shrimp-like crustaceans) in the nutrient-rich waters of Alaska and California all summer and autumn, Northern Humpback whales typically begin to arrive in Costa Rica sometime in December and remain visible in the area until around mid-April. Since some of the Northern Humpbacks spend their winter in Hawai'i, there are fewer whales to see in this migration, so your odds are a little lower than the peak season in July to November.

Whale Watching from July to November (Southern Humpback whales migrate north from Antarctica). Likewise, for the Southern Humpback whales, after eating their fill of nutritious krill all summer in the Southern Antarctic ocean (in the Southern hemisphere, winter and summer are reversed), these giant creatures travel all the way up north to Costa Rica. Southern Humpback whales typically arrive in the warm tropical waters around late July and remain visible in the area until around November. Since the humpback migration from Antarctica has the most whales, and their peak season in Costa Rica is between August and October, between these months, your odds of seeing a humpback are the best they'll ever be.

Whale Watching from mid-April to mid-July. There

typically aren't any humpback whales in the waters off of either of Costa Rica's shores during this time.

The Best Place to See Whales in Costa Rica

The Pacific coast is the best place to whale-watch, as it's where the numerous migrations of the Southern and Northern Humpbacks congregate. The North Atlantic Humpbacks migrate to the Caribbean coast, but as their numbers are far fewer, whale-watching isn't as popular on this coast. Although there is a possibility of seeing humpback whales along with many parts of Costa Rica's Pacific coastline, humpbacks tend to spend most of their time on the south stretch of the Pacific Costa Rican coast. Some of the best spots down here to see whales are the Osa Peninsula, Gulf of Dulce, Dominical, and Uvita.

As probably the most popular location to whale watch in the whole country, Uvita has a few extra wonderful features. First, the land, shoreline, and waters here are part of the Marino Ballena National Park (the National Whale Marine Park), spanning over 270 protected acres (110 hectares) of land and 13,200 acres (5,375 hectares) of protected ocean waters. As a safe, protected sanctuary, this area attracts many whales close to shore.

Second, Uvita is home to one of the most amazing, naturally occurring sand and rock formations - the Whale Tail! The Whale Tail is in the perfect shape of a whale's tail and juts out far from the beach straight into the ocean. The unique shape of the formation is caused by converging currents that deposit sand on top of rocks into this unique pattern. If you'd like to see it up close, you can walk all the way out to the point of the "tail." Check the tide charts before you go - you can only go on this little adventure at lower tides. Then, make your way to the main Marino Ballena National Park entrance in Uvita's Bahia neighborhood (there are two other entrances, so make sure you start at the right one), and pay a small admission (about $6USD for foreigners). Don't forget your hat, water, and sunscreen, as there is no shade, and it takes about 15-20 minutes to walk from the park ranger station to the tip of the "tail." And last but not least, don't forget your camera. There are many unique little tide pools on the way out, and you never know what kind of ocean life you might see.

Third, this funky, beautiful little town hosts the Annual Whale and Dolphin Festival during peak whale-watching season every year (typically sometime in early September). The famous festival features "short" two-hour whale and dolphin watching tours for half the price of an average, longer tour; there are live bands playing music and plenty of people dancing, each year, there is a beach run and mountain bike race, and there are always fun activities for children as well.

A Few Whale-y Fun Facts About These Amazing Ocean Creatures.

The humpback whale undertakes the longest migration of any mammal on Earth. Humpbacks often cover distances of up to 5,160 miles (8,300km), an incredible journey. And they can move surprisingly quickly, too - one humpback was recorded by NOAA (National Oceanic and Atmospheric Administration) as covering a 3,000 mile (4,830km) distance in just 36 days.

The humpback's main food source, tiny oceanic creatures called krill, are more numerous than perhaps the stars in the sky. To give you an idea, one species of krill, the Antarctic krill Euphausia superba, together have a biomass of over 379,000,000 tons (353,802,048,600kg)! That makes this species one of the top species, in terms of total biomass, on Earth. Wow.

During their entire migration, both male and female humpbacks don't feed at all. Because of this, nursing mothers can lose up to a third of their body weight during migration.

A baby humpback can already be as long as 13 to 16 feet (4-5m) at birth, and weigh up to 1 ton (907kg)! That's a big baby.

After about 11 months in the womb, baby humpbacks, called calves, are born. After birth, calves often stay by their mother's side for about a year. Bonus, heart-melting fact: mother and calf are often seen touching fins to show affection, almost like a loving fist bump.

Male humpbacks are nothing if not dedicated to romance. In

order to compete for a female, they sing elaborate songs, create detailed bubble displays, and physically fight one another for their chosen lady.

Adventures by Land: Activities & Sightseeing

Unlike some other tropical destinations, this country is not just about the beach. In fact, it's probably fair to say that when most travelers think of Costa Rica, they don't just dream about the beach: it's about 50/50 of ocean/land adventures here, making for an incredible amount of varied fun! I feel obligated to mention yet again that this is far from an exhaustive list of the land adventures you can discover in Costa Rica - it's just a summary of a few incredible highlights. Enjoy!

Walking & Hiking Through the Beautiful Landscapes of Costa Rica

You may be delighted to know that a handful of Costa Rica's most famous and popular trails all share a few key features: they are all very well maintained, stunningly beautiful, wildly different, provide a chance to view wildlife, and - for those of you looking for a lovely nature stroll vs. a full-on hike - they're all under two miles (3.2km). For the intrepid adventurers who are looking for a more challenging hike into the jungles, forests, and high country - there are plenty of options for you, too!

Many of these famous trails are often offered as guided nature walks; however, with the exception of the Sirena trail in Corcovado National Park, you can venture out on these well-traveled trails on your own. There are information pamphlets available at the entrance to each trail, and some trails even have signs alongside the trail that point out various plants, wildlife, or geographical features. The fact that these trails are famous might mean more crowds (depending on the season), but it's also kind of a guarantee of the quality you're getting - thousands upon thousands of people have walked these trails over the years to see some of the most incredible beauty and diverse flora and fauna that Costa Rica has to offer. Because there are many trails within each national park, I've listed the parks (or reserves) instead of the individual trails. Read on to learn more about some of the best walking and hiking adventures in Costa Rica.

Easy National Park & Reserve Nature Trails

Below are a few of the best maintained and easiest nature trails in Costa Rica: close to civilization and easily accessible/traversable for everyone.

Arenal Volcano National Park: Nature Walk Through Lava Fields

Location: Alajuela Province, Inland (Northern Central)

Approximate Park Size: 30,000 acres (12,150 hectares)

Hours Open: 8am - 4pm, daily

Entrance Fee: $10USD

Hike over old lava flows, through twisted volcanic landscapes, secondary rainforests, and a variety of other climates in this special park. Stop to get a detailed map at the entrance of the various winding trails throughout the park. Arenal Volcano National Park is the second most popular park in the country, with easy day trip access from the lovely town of nearby Fortuna (about 10 miles / 16km away).

The park features two dormant volcanoes. Volcano Arenal was suspected to be dormant for thousands of years, until one fateful day in 1968, when it erupted and destroyed several small towns, including the original town of Arenal. It has since been dormant. Volcano Chato, known as Cerro Chato, hasn't erupted for about 3,500 years; however, its last eruption created the beautiful little La Fortuna waterfall nearby, which is well worth going to see. There is also a gorgeous crater lake at the top of Cerro Chato! Hiking access for this volcano has been restricted for a few years, so be sure to ask before you go.

As in many trails in Costa Rica, there are ample opportunities to view wildlife on the trails of Arenal National Park, and if you're lucky, you might see any of the following: sloths, coatis (like a big, friendly raccoon), howler and spider monkeys, boa constrictors, deer, parrots, parakeets, black vultures, the extremely rare quetzal birds, and hummingbirds. There are many interesting and beautifully different types of flora as well.

Budget travelers' tip: FREE Arenal hot springs! Don't pay to go to the various hot springs in the area if you are on a tight budget. Instead, jump in a taxi and ask to go to "Rio Chollin," "Mini-Tabacon," or simply "the free hot springs." These hot springs aren't as fancy or as lovely as the ones you would pay for, and there are no lifeguards or amenities, but it is the same thermal water - and they won't lighten your wallet!

Manuel Antonio National Park: Amazing Wildlife, Steps Away from the Beach

Location: Puntarenas Province, mid-Pacific Coast

Approximate Park Size: 4,900 acres (1,983 hectares)

Hours Open: 7am - 4pm, closed Mondays

Entrance Fee: $16 USD (children under 12 are free)

Manuel Antonio might seem small for a national park, yet it's been named as one of the best parks in the world. You'll soon discover why as you step through the entrance, with monkeys swinging from the tree branches, frozen-looking sloths staring at you from high up, and the undergrowth scattered with the tiniest colorful rainforest frogs (you have to look really hard to find them). If the best thing about Manuel Antonio is the wildlife, the second best thing must be the incredibly easy access to see all of the wonders. Almost the entire trail is flat and well-maintained, making this a great option for family groups (think: grandma and grandson would both have no problem here) or for anyone looking to take a leisurely, manicured stroll through raw nature. It's an experience that is almost unrivaled with its easily accessible paths. That's not all, though - there are beaches here, too! Not one, but three lovely white sand beaches where you can actually take multiple swim and snorkel breaks on your walk. Don't forget your bathing suit and snorkel!

Monteverde Nature Reserves: Stroll Around in the Cloud Forests

Location: Puntarenas Province, Inland (Northern Central)

Approximate Reserve Sizes: Monteverde (26,000 acres / 10,500 hectares); Bosque Eterno de los Niños (55,800 hectares / 22,600 acres); Santa Elena (765 acres / 310 hectares).

Hours open: 7am – 4pm

Entrance fee: $16 adults, $7 children (Santa Elena); $25 adults, $12 children (Montverde); $15 adults, $10 children (Bosque Eterno de los Niños)

Ahhh, tropical cloud forests. Just the name "cloud forests" already sounds so dreamy. Well... the reality is that Costa Rica's tropical cloud forests *are* dreamily magical! First things first, though: what exactly is a cloud forest? The short answer is that it's a very wet forest on the slopes of a mountain in the clouds. Sometimes, cloud forests are even referred to as "water forests." Because cloud forests are usually located at higher elevations, they get a lot of rainfall year-round and have a persistent low-level cloud cover. Only 1% of the forests on Earth are considered cloud forests, making them incredibly rare. See? Magical.

And there's nothing quite like discovering the cloud forests from your absolutely lovely base camp of Monteverde. When I landed here, I'd already been traveling the warm, humid, and relatively "crowded" lowlands of Costa Rica for months. Arriving in the tiny mountain town of Monteverde, with its chill, peaceful vibes, and fresh mountain air after my long, hot travels, was a true pleasure, and I even gave a sigh of relief for a "vacation from my vacation." It felt great. If you have the time, set aside two or three days to explore this gorgeous national treasure! Get settled in your accommodation, and go out on an adventure every day. Note: while paying around $15-$25 USD might seem pricey for a nature walk, it stings a little less to know that a) you're seeing treasures that you cannot see anywhere else in the world, and b) most of that money goes back into maintaining the preserves and providing education about nature to visitors and local schools.

You have a few options here to see the different cloud forests of Monteverde. First, and by far the largest and most popular, is the Monteverde Cloud Forest Biological Reserve. The reserve is approximately 26,000 acres (10,500 hectares), a jaw-dropping 90% of which is virgin forest, or in other words, completely untouched. This reserve features hundreds upon hundreds of mammal, bird, reptilian, amphibian, and insect species, and has a particular claim to fame as being the region with the most species of orchids in the world (over 400).

Next up is the Bosque Eterno de los Niños or the Eternal Forest of the Children in English. Kind of a funny name, right? Incredibly, it is so named because the reserve was founded by donations from children in 44 different countries! It's a heartwarming story that is definitely worth going on an internet tangent to learn more. Amazingly, the reserve not only boasts similar amounts of pristine flora and fauna to the Monteverde Reserve, but it also provides water for hundreds of nearby farms and communities, in addition to water for hydroelectric projects that produce more than a third of Costa Rica's electricity. This reserve is a whopping 55,800 acres of 22,600 hectares. Wow. Nice job, kids!

And last, but definitely not least, is my personal favorite: the smallest of them all, the Santa Elena Cloud Forest Reserve. At just 765 acres (310 hectares), and only 4 miles (7km) from the town of Monteverde, this less visited, easily accessible reserve felt to me like a private little wonderland. While the trails are much shorter, you still have a better chance of being completely alone in nature, which naturally increases your chances of spotting wildlife. I like to daydream in the solitude and peace of raw nature in these settings, and this reserve was perfect for it. Plus, when I took a little lunch break, gazing around at my beautiful surroundings, I saw a hummingbird "taking a shower" in the tiniest of "waterfalls" (the waterfall was only about 3 ft. / 1m high). The hummingbird peacefully flitted in and out of the water over and over with a majestic backdrop of teeming jungle greenery, and I have to say, that's one of the most magical things I've ever seen.

More Challenging National Park Nature Trails

Below are a few of the best challenging nature trails in Costa Rica: a little off the beaten path, a little harder to get to, a lot harder to complete, and totally worth it.

Chirripó National Park: Hike the Mt. Everest of Costa Rica in the Clouds

Location: San José, Limón and Cartago Provinces, Inland (Southern Central)

Approximate Park Size: 125,650 acres (50,849 hectares)

Hours Open: 5:30am - 5pm, daily

Entrance Fee: $18

The entrance to this park is almost as fun as the park itself, for me. The tiny mountain town of San Gerardo de Rivas is nestled high up in the foothills of the mountain range, and as soon as you step off the bus, you can feel the difference in temperature and air quality: the air is crisp and fresh and delightfully cool. There's no exaggerating here; the town is truly tiny, with just a few restaurants and several accommodations and some proud and friendly townfolk. Make sure you check out how far your accommodation is from the town center and from the park entrance before you book - the town is all steep hills and very sharp inclines, so even though your hostel might be "only a quarter mile from town," that is a heck of a walk.

This gigantic park holds quite a few records: it's the coldest place in Costa Rica, it's the third-largest park in the country, and the peak of Cerro Chirripó Grande is the 38th most prominent peak in the world - and the highest peak in all of Central America - at 12,533ft (3,820m). If you want to hike overnight to the summit, you will need to undertake a little extra planning - a permit and reservation are required, and there is limited space, so make sure you book months in advance.

Though the park is made up of many different climates or ecosystems (including a "wet desert," fern groves - with Lomaria ferns as tall as you, madrono forests, and more), its two main climates are primary rainforest and cloud forest. Temperatures in the park are much lower than the rest of the country and can range widely, from 18°C (64° F) to 26° C (79° F)

In the lower regions, temperatures can drop to 0° C (32° F) to 12° C (54° F) in the highlands. Nights can be very cold and foggy, and during the day, the temperature can change rapidly from sunny to clouds to drizzle to bitterly cold winds exceeding 50mph (80kph). Be very sure you have packed well if you plan to visit and hike here because you'll need items you probably won't need anywhere else in Costa Rica (see our "What to Pack" chapter towards the end of this book).

The name Chirripó means "Land of the Eternal Waters." If you hike here in the rainy season, dozens and dozens of streams and brooks will reveal themselves. If you're brave (and fit) enough to take on the 11 mile (17.7km) hike to the summit - many a hiker's lifelong dream - you'll have a spectacular, sweeping view of the surrounding landscapes (including over 30 lakes and lagoons in the wet season, many of which don't exist in the dry season). The park boasts over 260 species of amphibians and reptiles, 400 bird species (including the incredibly rare quetzal), the largest population of tapirs in the country, peccaries, monkeys, puma jaguars, and many more.

Pro tip: Not feeling up to the wild challenge of summiting the Costa Rican Mt. Everest? Or maybe you are, but the hike permits were sold out for the time you'll be there? Never fear! The outrageously beautiful and peaceful Cloudbridge Nature Reserve is literally right next door, with the entrance easily reached on foot from the tiny town. The story of how the reserve was founded is beautiful (civilians banded together to restore 700 acres (283 hectares) of dried-out cattle lands to the original montane forest), and with an entrance fee of just $7 (free for children under 16), opening hours from sunrise to sunset, and miles of self-guided trails, Cloudbridge Reserve is truly a hidden gem just waiting for you to discover.

Corcovado National Park - Biodiversity & Incredible Wildlife

Location: Puntarenas Province, Osa Peninsula (Southern Pacific Coast)

Approximate Park Size: 726,000 acres (293,802 hectares)

Hours Open: 7am - 4pm, daily (Sirena section is closed for the month of October)

Entrance Fee: $15USD; $5USD for children aged 2-12; free for children under 2 and seniors over 65

Corcovado is a name that you will hear uttered often with the deepest respect on your travels in Costa Rica. There are over

140 mammal species, 370 bird species, and 10,000 insect species in the biggest park in Costa Rica - an incredible 2.5% of the entire planet's biodiversity! National Geographic aptly called it "the most biologically intense place on Earth." It seems almost like a secret, magical land, so far removed from all of the other attractions of this country as to almost be on another planet. Not to mention, due to the extremely remote nature of its location on the Osa Peninsula (southern Pacific coast), not many travelers ever actually make it to Corcovado. If you want to experience the wonder, you have to do a bit of extra planning and traveling to get here. And it is so worth it. Wildlife greatly outnumbers the humans here for a unique experience you'll never forget.

You'll find five different sections in the park: Sirena, Los Patos, Leona, El Tigre, and San Pedrillo. Many visitors to the park do day trip hikes to Sirena and San Pedrillo and enjoy themselves immensely. However, those who wish to venture even further into the wild undertake the 8.6 mile (14km) overnight trail from Leona to Sirena. It's not for the faint of heart. The trail will take you deep into the jungles and rainforest, crossing rivers that just might have crocodiles or even sharks at high tide, and if you're lucky, you'll see the likes of tapirs, wild pigs, squirrel monkeys, white-faced capuchin monkeys, howler monkeys, spider monkeys, margay spotted wildcat, macaws, sloths, friendly coatis (kinda like big raccoons), cute little agoutis (they look like tiny pigs), and so much more. If you are extremely lucky, you might even see the very rare puma wildcat.

Tenorio Volcano National Park: See the Wonders of the Celeste Waterfall & Hanging Bridges

Location: Guanacaste Province, Inland (Northern Central)

Approximate Park Size: 31,794 acres (12,866 hectares)

Hours Open: 8am - 4pm, daily (last admission in is at 2pm)

Entrance Fee: $12

The most popular draw of this park is undoubtedly the heavenly light blue waters of the enchanting Rio Celeste or Celeste River. When you see the photos online, you may wave it aside as photoshopped, but when you see them in person, I promise you will gasp in awe. As per usual, there is no real magic here, just some very cool science: the unearthly blue waters are caused by the natural emanation of sulfur and the precipitation of calcium carbonates. Fun science jargon for "extremely beautiful."

Before I go any further, it's important to note that swimming in this park is prohibited, unfortunately, and that includes

Rio Celeste. The hike in to see the river is a little challenging, as are the other hikes in this park, so be prepared.

There are two volcanoes here, the Tenorio Volcano and the Montezuma Volcano, both dormant. The rest of the park is covered in primary cloud forest and rainforest and is absolutely full of different plants and wildlife - are you seeing a pattern here in Costa Rica? There is incredible life crammed into every corner of this country, and it is a wonder to behold. Tenorio Volcano Park also boasts many other lovely rivers and waterfall, authentic hot springs, and more, including:

> The Laguna La Danta (Tapir Lake): a crater lake at the summit of Tenorio Volcano! The lake is a jewel, named after the animals that stop here often to drink water. The hike to the lake/summit is for experienced hikers only.

> The Hanging Bridges of Bijagua, also known as the Heliconias Hanging Bridges Trail: on the fringes of the park lies the peaceful little town of Bijagua and the Heliconias Ecolodge, which is owned and operated by the local community. The trails here are in the middle elevation forest and are a birders' heaven, along with many other types of wildlife. The lodge charges $10 to

use their trails.

Important Notes for Any Trail Adventure

Whether you are planning to undertake a walking or hiking trail, guided or unguided, there are a few basic rules that can mean the difference between life and death. It sounds like a joke if you're reading this in the gentle sea breezes at the beach or from the comfort of your bedroom, but it sounds less funny when you realize that at least one person gets lost hiking in Costa Rica every year, never to be seen again. So! Remember these trusty trail rules - they're most important if you're planning unguided hikes, but smart to remember for any nature hike:

1. Never go solo, unless you are a very experienced hiker.

2. Always let someone know where you're going and your estimated return time.

3. Carry extra water and food (that means take more than you think you'll need).

4. Take a printed map and also download your route to your smartphone or GPS before leaving Wi-Fi (so you can access it when offline).

5. Bring a warm layer - yep, you read that right. It's always smart to bring a rain jacket, flannel, or sweater with you. It's hard to believe, but hypothermia can be a big problem if you get lost overnight in a wet, chilly rainforest.

Do You Have a Budget Yet? Here Are 11 Easy Tips to Save Your Money

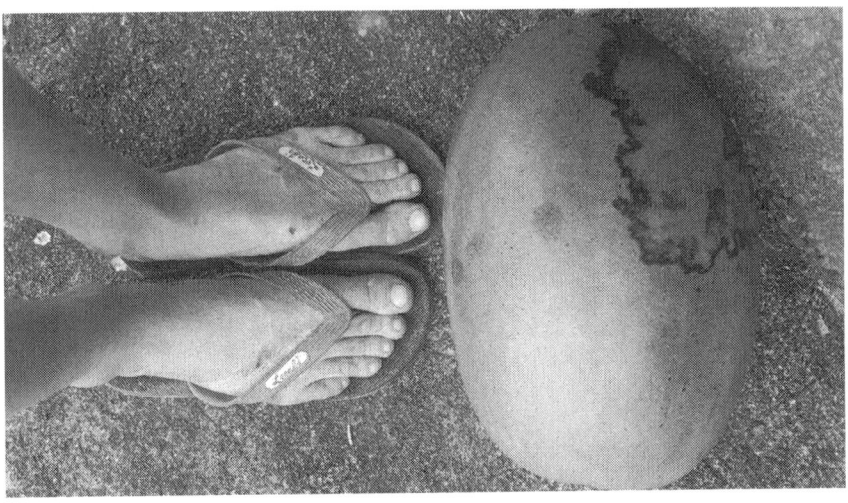

Costa Rica is known as the most modern, safe Central American country compared to its neighbors. Infrastructure such as accommodations, medical, education, and transportation are all easily accessible, reliable, and there are, more often than not, options of good quality. Traveling throughout the country is relatively safe, whether you are a large group, family, or solo traveler. The country maintains a high level of eco-minded sustainability in its government, commercial activities, and attitudes of its people that are rarely found elsewhere in poorer countries. Costa Rica is also home to a thriving, creative, and well-established expatriate community.

For all of these quality trademarks and more, as the old saying goes, you really do get what you pay for. In other words, Costa Rica can be a bit expensive for the budget traveler. That is unless you have insider information! I have gathered all of the best money-saving tips that I've learned personally and that I have learned from others, and summarized them neatly for you below. If you can follow even a few of these suggestions, you are guaranteed to save a hefty amount of your savings (that you can put towards your next adventure). And an organized, well-established country has its money-saving aspects, as well - it's rare to find a spot in Costa Rica where you can't drink clean water straight from the faucet (saving you money on bottled water), and the minimal crime factor saves you a lot of money in potential scams or robberies.

Don't Eat Every Meal Out

You'll soon find that the bulk of your spending will likely be in the food and drink sector of your Costa Rica vacation (aside from accommodation). One way to mitigate this is to cook a few meals of your own now and then (and choose lodging that accommodates cooking, like a hostel, for example). Purchasing food in the grocery stores can be expensive, too, depending on your location and what you are buying, but with a little patience, you can come up with a cheap meal that can be replicated a few times on your trip. For example, tuna salad and crackers, tacos, porridge, pasta, or peanut butter and jelly, all fairly cheap at the supermarket. If you're lucky enough to get a two-week tropical vacation and decide to make your own meal once a day, that could be around $150 - $200USD or more of savings! The same goes for your alcoholic drinks - if you plan on a night out, drink a beer or have a glass of wine at your hotel or hostel before heading out to save money, or take a little cooler with you to the beach during the day with snacks and drinks. If you're an espresso drink fan, making your coffee at your rental will save you quite a bit of money, too.

Eat at the Local Soda

When you do eat out, consider frequenting the local "Sodas" or mom-and-pop type "diner" restaurants found everywhere in the country. For one thing, they will give you the true, delicious flavor and cozy local vibe of Costa Rica. And for another, they will treat your wallet very, very nicely - a big casado plate (a mixed plate with rice, beans, vegetables, plantains, and a protein like chicken, fish, or beef) for dinner will only set you back a few dollars, whereas eating Italian,

American, or Thai food might cost you closer to $12USD. Plus, this way, you support a local Costa Rican family! Another option is to look for the local Musmanni bakery chain found almost everywhere in the country. They usually have a great lunch special with a soda for under $3USD, and pastries for around $1USD.

Don't Book in Advance

Don't book your tours ahead of time or on the internet. This may seem counter-intuitive, as many companies advertise sales and their "best prices" online. But the companies that can afford to maintain expensive websites and sales representatives are probably not the cheapest companies around, and their target market is someone who wants to spend more than you do. You can very often find a better deal asking around in person. A great way to get around this is to just book one or two nights ahead of time, and then ask around when you arrive.

Ask for Discounts

Ask for a discount when you do splurge and book tours, classes, or excursions, rent gear, or are purchasing a ticket for a long private car or shuttle ride. If you are traveling in a group, ask for a discount. If you're a solo traveler, but you know you're going to rent a surfboard for, say, five days in a row, ask for a discount. If they decline your request, be respectful, and accept it - unlike some Latin American countries, Costa Ricans don't particularly like to haggle or negotiate. But it never hurts to ask! I have easily saved hundreds of dollars on vacation by simply asking.

Only Hire a Guide if Necessary

Don't book a guide if you don't really have to. Sometimes, a guide adds serious quality to your experience or even safety, or they may be mandatory for the adventure you've chosen (such as scuba diving). But at other times, they really aren't necessary to have a good time. A great example of this is the incredible nature walks offered throughout the beautiful Manuel Antonio National Park on the south Pacific coast. You can view much of Costa Rica's tropical wildlife up close and personal while walking through verdant jungles and stopping by white sand beaches and azure waters, an experience that is unmatched in many countries - it's really unique. However, as soon as you pay your park admission fee, you will be inundated with offers of a guide. The park guides carry expensive camera scopes and can point out some wildlife that you might miss spotting on your own (like the tiniest of rare treefrogs), but honestly, you can see much of what the park has to offer without paying an extra $20USD per person. Think of it this way - if you try the non-guided option and feel like you missed out, you can always just go back and pay for a guide.

Ask a Local Instead

Alternatively, consider asking a local to be your guide or take you on a tour. Many times, a local Tico or Tica will either be able to take you themselves or know a friend or family member who can take you on your adventure as a guide. You'll be supporting a local family, and likely making a new friend. For example, if you want to go fishing but don't want to pay the steep prices of an expensive deep-sea fishing tour, try asking your nearest Costa Rican if they know anyone with a boat. If you are a solo traveler, try asking someone in your hostel or hotel if they would like to accompany you on your local adventure - it's always safer to go in a small group. Never go out alone with a stranger.

Travel in the Off-Season

Book your trip in the off-season between May and December. If you're not afraid of a little rain (translation: sometimes a LOT of rain), you can save bucket loads of money by planning your trip in the off-season. As mentioned earlier in the book, it really depends on where you are in the country as to how much rainfall you'll actually have to deal with. Just a little bit of research can save you a lot of money, and to be on the safe, less-rainy side, you can always book on the ends, or shoulders, of the season - so, in May, early June, late November, and December.

Ride the Bus

Utilize the well-established public transportation system of buses. Well-established doesn't mean fancy - many buses are not air-conditioned (though many of them are); if you choose a particularly busy route on a busy time/day at the last minute, you might be forced to go "solo de pies" or "standing room only," and there are no bathrooms on the bus for long journeys (but they do make regular stops every two hours or so for restrooms and snacks), etc.

Still, it's your best option for transportation as a budget traveler, and odds are you will most likely even enjoy yourself. There's something to be said for staring out the window at all of the beautiful countrysides slowly passing by, traveling as the locals do, and very likely meeting new friends along the way. You'll save a lot of dollars by eschewing the more touristic and expensive taxis and private shuttles that can cost you a pretty penny in the blink of an eye.

Stay at a Hostel

Stay in hostel dorms. If you don't mind sharing your space with other like-minded travelers, you will save yourself a great deal of money. Not only are hostel dorms much cheaper (sometimes as little as $8USD), but they offer you a communal kitchen option, where you can cook a few of your own meals, talk with some fellow travelers, and save even more money.

Plus, pro tip - many hostels have a "free food" drawer in the cupboard and/or refrigerator, so be sure to ask. Travelers who find they have bought too much food for their stay and don't want to waste it upon their departure will often leave perfectly good loaves of bread, unopened packets of pasta or rice, fruit, condiments, tortillas, and more, to share with others.

Don't Buy Bottled Water

Bring your reusable water bottle with you. If you can remember to always fill your reusable water bottle when you are near a tap, you will save yourself some great money (and the environment!) by not buying bottled water. Water in Costa Rica is safe to drink from the tap in almost every location (be sure to double-check if you are in a more remote or hard-to-get-to location - for example, Santa Teresa - as their water source is often a private well or tank).

Consider Alternative Types of Accommodation

Try researching the many work-for-trade, cultural exchange, or volunteer options around the country. One of my absolute favorite websites is Workaway.info, an internationally well-respected organization that facilitates cultural exchange, working holiday, and volunteering opportunities in every corner of Costa Rica (and all of the other countries in the world, as well).

It will cost you about $40USD for membership, but it's well worth it, and you will save that $40 many times over if you choose to go this route. Before you pay a membership fee, you are allowed to view all of the different host opportunities available where you are traveling, so you know what you'll be paying for (membership allows you to then safely contact the host).

This is one of the best ways to see the "real" side of Costa Rica, working alongside other travelers, locals, or even staying with a Costa Rican family. All hosts offer some type of lodging in exchange for a certain amount of hours of work per week (sometimes as low as 15 hours, sometimes as high as 40 hours), many hosts also offer some type of board/food/meals as well, and a select few even offer pay.

As an example, I stayed with a Costa Rican Workaway host that was a surfing hostel right on the beach. In exchange for a few hours of work 5 days a week (mostly reception and making sure the kitchen was tidy), I received a free dorm bed and free breakfast. Awesome!

Need a Place to Stay? The Best Budget Accommodations

One of the many advantages of a well-established country in Central America is the varied options of accommodation everywhere you go. No matter where you are in the country, there is almost always a high-end, luxury option, a very comfortable mid-range option, an economical no-frills option, and a lower end real-budget type option. Accommodation in Costa Rica varies from resorts, boutique hotels, larger hotel chains, small mom-and-pop type motels, hostels of all shapes and kinds from low end to rather fancy high end, cabins, villas, Airbnb, and camping, to even Couchsurfing. You can take your pick! Of course, if you're traveling on a budget, your best bet will always be hostel dorms, very cheap hotels, work-for-trade, or Couchsurfing - all easily found with a quick search online. Below you'll find a brief description of the best budget accommodation types and a shortlist of some of my absolute favorite and affordable places that I've personally stayed in around the country.

Hostels and Budget Motels/Hotels

It's always wise to have at least one night of accommodation booked before you arrive in a new town, but just be wary of online prices, and know that you are almost guaranteed to find a cheaper option by walking around your new town and asking in person. This is partly because many smaller hostels and hotels are not listed on the main accommodation sites such as Hostels.com, Hostelbookers.com, or Booking.com, and/or can't afford a fancy website with good SEO.

Work-for-Trade

One of the most popular and well-established work-for-trade websites is called Workaway.info, with "hosts" all over the country. Workaway took an idea that is as old as time - trade

- and honed it to a world traveler's perfection, allowing budget travelers a glimpse into their chosen destination that would be difficult to get on a "normal" vacation. Workaway "hosts" are either individuals or businesses who would like you to stay with them for anywhere from a couple of days to a few months, helping out with whatever work or project they currently have going on. In exchange for a few hours of work each day (each host varies), you receive a free bed, sometimes even a private room, and sometimes there is a free daily meal thrown in as well. Very rarely, you will find a host willing to even compensate you monetarily as well (but then you have to worry about work visas).

Couchsurfing

Couchsurfing.com, in case you didn't know, is a "global homestay and social networking service." The term "couch surfing," of course, is a verb that was invented to describe sleeping on in other people's homes - most often, on their couches - as a type of accommodation when traveling. The concept is an old one. People have been sleeping on other people's couches (or straw mats) since the beginning of time. But Couchsurfing.com took it a step further in the 1990s and created a global hub for hosts and travelers to connect and provide a measure of safety and security for those interested in doing so with their vetting and feedback protocols.

Couchsurfing is technically the cheapest way to travel because you don't pay anything or have to provide any kind of service as payment, but it does come with a price: risk.

Many, many travelers and backpackers the world over have stayed in all kinds of homes in every kind of culture, making new friends and even sometimes meeting the love of their life (some crazy people use this site for dating, but that is quite dangerous, to be honest). Like everything free, though, this service comes with a warning - do your research and remember you are staying with complete strangers. You will literally be at the mercy of the foreign person whose home you are staying in. The site does make a good effort to vet their hosts, of course, with reviews you can read from other travelers, but it is still always a big gamble, especially if you are a solo traveler and/or female. Make sure your host has plenty of positive feedback. Don't ever stay with a host that has no feedback or negative feedback; it's not worth the risk. And always, always make sure your loved ones know exactly when and where you are staying with a Couchsurfing host. But if you've done your research and feel comfortable with the host you've chosen, enjoy the (free) adventure!

Six of My Favorite Costa Rican Accommodations

On my travels to this lovely country over the years, there have been a few standout accommodations where I've made memories and friends I'll never forget. Sometimes, when you travel, you're lucky enough to find an accommodation that is uniquely wonderful: maybe they have incredibly friendly and helpful staff that make you feel like you're at home, you can't believe the incredible value/bargain prices, you feel very safe and secure even in a foreign neighborhood, and/or the location is just perfect for embarking on incredible local adventures.

Most of my favorite places listed below boast all of the above, and more. Fun fact: several of the wonderful owners have agreed to provide a discount on your stay with them if you mention your trusty Costa Rican Budget Travel Guide!

Hostel La Posada - Affordable, Friendly, Beach Vibes

Santa Teresa, Nicoya Peninsula, Puntarenas Province

"You're in the right place!" That's the message that pops up when you visit this colorful hostel's website, and if you're a budget traveler looking for beauty off the beaten path, they're absolutely right. This international surf camp and hostel sits just a few steps from the infamously beautiful beach of Santa Teresa. The bustling little town of Santa Teresa stretches out over a few miles, hugging the coastline and backed by dense jungle that rises up a hill (a great spot to enjoy an aerial view of the sunset and perfect waves stretching out in every direction). As such, it's a very long walk from one side of town to the other.

Hostel La Posada enjoys being right in the center of activity, close to a supermarket, local Soda, surfboard and ATV rentals, and many buzzing local restaurants, bars, and even a few dance clubs. The hostel itself is owned and managed by two best friends, Guillermo "Guille" (pronounced "ghee-zjhay") from Uruguay and Jeronimo from Argentina. Guille and Jeronimo love Costa Rica, their hostel, and what they do with a passion - and that shines through the welcome you'll receive at Hostel La Posada and your all-over experience during your stay there. The laid-back, smiling staff will bend over backward to help you book an activity or plan an adventure. The hostel is not fancy - it is a budget accommodation, after all - but it's beautifully decorated by both local and international artists, and effortlessly creates a friendly, hip atmosphere. You're just as likely to be invited to a home-cooked meal or amiable game of pool (billiards) or ping pong (my favorite!) with the crew or guests in the hostel's cozy lounge and dining area, as you are to be regaled with amazing live music from a local or traveling musician.

Like the laws of attraction dictate, the hostel seems to attract people just as kind, fun-loving, and creative as their hosts. The hostel also has its own sparkling pool and hammocks for those lazy afternoons. I had some of my favorite memories in Costa Rica here - surfing every morning and afternoon, eating at the local Soda, and visiting the gorgeous tide pools at sunset with new friends from the hostel. You can find out more on their website, www.laposadasantateresa.com. AND, you can mention this book to receive a 10% discount on your stay at La Posada Hostel!

Lake Arenal Hotel & Brewery (LAB) - Stunning Views, Good Food, Peaceful Nature

Lake Arenal (off the highway near the town of Tilarán), Guanacaste Province

"Good Food. Good Beer. Good Times." That's the simple slogan of this tranquil oasis, and it's more than enough for the weary traveler looking for a peaceful place to set a spell. What LAB does, though, it does very well. It's a unique experience unlike any other, as you can probably tell by visiting their website. The renovated hotel retains its prior dignity and quiet class, with a distinctly novel feel throughout the grounds - there are lovely frescoes of native histories on the walls, a grand entrance, and palatial stairs that lead down to a gorgeous pool area with a separate pool room for the jacuzzi area (featuring more amazing art and the most lovely, unique jacuzzi I've ever had the pleasure of relaxing in).

The hotel isn't even the main attraction, though. The owner, JP, a quick-talking, friendly U.S. ex-pat with a perpetual twinkle in his eyes, created a brewery downstairs that uses local grains, secret recipes, and crystal clear pure water trickling down the slopes of the nearby volcano. Ask nicely, and JP will take you on a grand tour of the brewery at almost any time of day. He knows his equipment, processes, and history intimately, is very passionate about his craft, and his enthusiasm is contagious, which makes the tour fascinating and fun. And of course, you are treated with a taste of his favorite beers - made on-site! - throughout the tour. LAB gets a lot of extra points for not only being a great option for accommodation and entertainment (they host regular live music at night when the dining area and bar come alive) but also for being incredibly sustainable. The hotel and brewery actually sit on a 15-acre (about 6 hectares) organic farm, which supplies the restaurant with fresh dairy and vegetables. You are allowed to stroll through the lovely, sweeping gardens and jungle anytime, and even the farm if you ask for a guide, and the lake itself is only a ten-minute walk away (although it's not suitable for swimming).

While the hotel rooms aren't exactly expensive, they're not necessarily affordable for the budget traveler, either. But, pro tip - ask for a bed in one of their lesser-known cozy dorm rooms! The dorm rooms are often empty, so you might have the place to yourself, plus they feature a fireplace and sliding glass doors to the perfectly manicured lawn and jungle just behind it, and the lake beyond that - first-class accommodation for a dorm room. To top it all off, the staff are warm-hearted and quick with a smile, truly making you feel like you are right at home. I loved every one of them, and treasured my peaceful time here (I got so much writing done!). You can visit their website www.lakearentalhotel.com for more information. Mention this guide to receive a 20% discount.

Pura Vida Hostel - Affordable, Great Vibes, Good Music

Tamarindo, Nicoya Peninsula, Guanacaste Province

When you visit Tamarindo yourself, you will find that for

every few steps you take, there is a different hostel or hotel to choose from. The selection can be a bit overwhelming at times, to be honest. While there are plenty of great options to choose from, personally, the Pura Vida Hostel stands out to me for their affordability, cleanliness, friendly vibes from multilingual staff, and best of all - their genuinely chilled out atmosphere and amazing live music and entertainment all week long. Again, while the accommodation itself is nothing fancy, it's the great feeling of the place that sets it apart from the pack, and it is always clean, safe, and friendly. You can choose from very affordable bunk dorms, private rooms, and even larger private rooms to share with friends or family. You can even choose rooms with or without A.C., and save money accordingly. Pura Vida Hostel's motto is: "Come as a Guest, Leave as a Friend," and that was certainly true for me. Though I'd only planned to stay here for three days, I ended up staying for two weeks because it was such a great, cozy, and friendly vibe.

The "rancho," or lounge area, dominates the center of the hostel and features hammocks, daybeds, couches, and rocking chairs for you to relax on. The lounge area looks into a small but lovely tropical garden with more tables and chairs. Almost every night, everyone gathers around this center, taking a seat wherever there's space, making friends, and enjoying the local creative art and/or music being played for their entertainment. In terms of convenience, the hostel is located right next door to a heavenly French bakery, across the street from a bank, and only a couple of blocks away from the vibrant weekend markets in one direction and the stunning Tamarindo beaches in the other direction. You can find out more by visiting their website, www.puravidahostel.com. AND you can mention this book to receive a 20% discount on your stay at Pura Vida Hostel!

Tranqui Funkey Cabinas

Playa Avellana, Guanacaste Province

Tranqui Funkey is a delightfully designed, hip little surf and yoga village located just 30 minutes south of bustling Tamarindo. The "village" is a short five or ten-minute walk (depending which route you take) to the lovely long stretch of beach. Playa Avellana (Avellana Beach), also known as "Little Hawai'i," is a secret known among surf circles for the incredibly well-formed and large swells that roll in here - truly a surfer's paradise. It's a wild place, far from the noisy, busy cities, offering beautiful tan sand, mangrove trees providing shade not far from the shore, and crystal clear waters. I've enjoyed some of the incredible shell collecting in the world here! It is not only gorgeous but also very peaceful, just the way the friendly locals like it. Tranqui Funkey has everything you need: beautifully decorated private rooms or "cabinas" equipped with icy cold AC, hot water, private parking space, and a private hammock. There's an open-air kitchen, a very large wooden deck built above the kitchen (with more hammocks) for yoga, meditation, or to simply relax, a BBQ area, flowers everywhere, even a lovely tiny bar and organic restaurant. It's not uncommon to see local ranchers herding their peaceful Brahman cattle down the road, or to wake up to the funny growls of a 12-member family of howler monkeys in the tree branches high above you (the babies are extremely cute).

As you gently sway to and fro in your hammock, you can

decide which way you'll walk down to the beach later. You can head to the left on the road, pass through a little resort area, and stroll along a gorgeous wooden walkway that is built above a sweeping mangrove - it's very unique and quite magical as you walk through a beautiful alien landscape to arrive at the beach. Or, you can head to the right on the road, down to the popular restaurant and bar with their friendly faces - this is the main entrance to the beach.

As their name suggests, this little surf and yoga village is both tranquil and funky, just like its happy multilingual Italian owner, Nicola, and his best friend, a sweet dog named Amigo. Tranqui Funkey offers yoga classes and surf lessons and will help you book horseback riding trips on the beach or in the jungle, fishing trips on a boat, stand-up paddleboarding (SUP) on the river, and more. Their prices aren't as low as a hostel, but you can score a double-room cabin in the offseason for just $50 - and this is still my favorite place to splash out, budget style. Plus, they are big on sustainability, another win. You can visit their website http://www.tranquifunkey.com for more information or email tranquifunkey@gmail.com. AND, you can mention this book for a 10% discount on your stay at Tranqui Funkey!

Five More Honorable Mentions

Here are a few more of my favorite places to stay in different locations around the country. I don't have space to list every single wonderful business I've encountered on my travels through Costa Rica, but these lodgings deserve mention because they are kind hosts, clean, safe, affordable, close to some of the best adventures nearby, and I can personally vouch for their quality.

Casa Mariposa

San Gerardo de Rivas, San José Province (at the base of

Cerro Chirripó)

This is a wonderfully unique and incredibly beautiful lodge nestled in a tiny mountain town, conveniently close to the entrance of Cerro Chirripó National Park and also the entrance to Cloudbridge Nature Reserve. This area is a little slice of heaven on Earth - you'll never have seen anything like it. Plus, they have a strong focus on sustainability (www.casamariposachirripo.net).

Cool Vibes Hostel

Dominical, Puntarenas Province

Their motto is "Stay, Relax, Enjoy," and this is exactly what this hostel offers - cozy, affordable accommodations, very friendly staff for a great price, a huge shared kitchen and living room, and a tiny pool. Plus, it's only steps away from the beach (www.hosteldominical.com).

Hotel Casa Tago

Alajuela, San José, San José Province

This lovely little family hotel is an oasis in the busy neighborhoods of Alajuela (a kind of "city-within-a-city" located in San José that is conveniently close to the airport).

It has a gorgeous pool, private rooms with flat-screen TVs, free breakfast, and a 24hr front desk (www.hotelcasatago.com).

Wide Mouth Frog Hostel

Quepos, Puntarenas Province

This is a well-done little backpackers' hostel in the transit town of Quepos - you'll likely stop here at some point if you travel south along the Pacific Coast. The hostel boasts friendly staff, tropical gardens, a large pool, a shared kitchen, an on-site restaurant, gated grounds, and a lot of good vibes.

Flutterby House

Uvita, Puntarenas Province

This unique place is an eco-friendly hostel with an on-site bar and restaurant. It's beautiful and definitely different! Be prepared to climb a ladder into a "treehouse" if you choose the dorm option. It has a beautiful kitchen and yoga deck (www.flutterbyhouse.com).

Five of the Best Ways to Get Around Costa Rica

If you are a budget traveler, there's no question about it: the best way to get around Costa Rica is by bus. The Costa Rican public transportation system is affordable, reliable, comfortable, easy to navigate with the right information, with buses that frequently run all throughout the country. Because Costa Rican buses operate on set routes and scheduled timetables, they are very dependable, which is why they are the main mode of transportation for most locals.

Even if you weren't traveling on a budget, I still highly recommended it - there's something so relaxing and calming about giving up control of your holiday for a moment to your friendly bus driver, as they cruise around the gorgeous countryside, fresh breeze blowing in your window (or sometimes, icy cold air conditioning), and you're almost guaranteed to make a new friend on your journey. When you know you'll be on board for a few hours, you're almost forced to relax. I love to read, write in my journal, nap, and even snap photos of the pretty views outside my bus window.

The main drawback of using Costa Rican buses as your primary mode of transportation is that they are slow going. You can expect to be on a bus for up to eight hours pretty regularly if you plan to travel all the way around the country. If you're in a hurry or don't have that long to vacation, you may want to consider mixing up your transportation options so that you take a few taxis, shuttles, and flights as well. Though it will cost you quite a bit more, it may be worth it to have that extra day or two at your favorite beach, peaceful mountain jungle, or vibrant city. There are also private bus options (a company called Gray Line is probably the most popular) that will cost you closer to $40 - $80USD for a public bus ride that would cost you $3 - $20USD. An important note to keep in mind no matter what transportation option you choose is the phone number to dial for any emergency in Costa Rica - it's the same as the United States, and easy to remember: 911.

Bus

The secret to traveling by bus is to have the right information in terms of a comprehensive bus schedule, plan your bus trip ahead of time (allowing for a little flexibility on either side - you never know if there will be a rare traffic jam or breakdown), and to ask locals a lot of questions whenever you are unsure of something. Ticos and Ticas are very friendly and helpful and seem to find pride in assisting foreigners in navigating their country.

The best bus schedule for Costa Rica is available to download as a PDF from Costa Rica's official tourism website (here is the link: www.visitcostarica.com/en/costa-rica/bus-itinerary). For some reason, throughout all of my travels in Costa Rica and all of the new friends I made, no one ever told me about this schedule. I had to find it on my own, and breathed a huge sigh of relief when I did... it's true that the locals are friendly and helpful, but remembering a long list of bus stops and transfers in a foreign language is tricky, to say the least. More often than not, people will just help you with one leg of your journey, and you'll have to keep asking every time you get to a new stop.

To that end, you'll definitely want to print out a copy of this before you leave home, and save the PDF to your phone as well for easy access. It takes just a minute or two to understand the layout of the schedule, with the following clearly noted: name of arrival city, departure terminal, service frequency, return schedule from different locations, and even travel time and distance traveled in kilometers. The service rates are not included, but you can expect to pay around $3USD for shorter rides, and around $20USD for full-day trips. Another great bonus of the Costa Rica Tourism bus schedule is that it includes the country's ferry, boat, train, and Central American bus service schedules.

As mentioned, many travelers don't know about this public bus schedule and end up relying on piecemeal information from various sources that makes traveling by bus a little more difficult. With this schedule in hand, you really can't go wrong - just remember that during the end of year holidays and Easter weekend, everything changes and is generally less available, so be extra careful to plan ahead at these times of the year. As always, be sure to keep a close eye on your luggage and belongings. Oftentimes, your larger luggage will be stowed underneath the bus, and for longer trips, they will give you a little luggage receipt, which is great. Keep your smaller bags close to you while you are on the bus. It's always best to pay for smaller transactions, including bus tickets, in colones, so remember to keep a stash of smaller bill colones on you at all times while you travel through Costa Rica.

Taxis

Unless you're really strapped for cash, taxis are probably the best way to quickly and conveniently get around the bigger cities and towns. Taxis won't be as available in smaller or more remote towns, so it's smart to call and book ahead of time in these places if you know you'll need a taxi (save a few taxi company phone numbers in your phone for each new location you visit - you can get these from your local accommodation). City taxis run by the meter and generally will charge you about $2USD as a base fare and an additional $2 for every mile traveled. Later at night (around 9 or 10pm), prices go up.

Always check to make sure your taxi's meter is running when you get in the vehicle - sometimes, a dishonest taxi driver will try to charge you more if they "forget" to turn on their meter. If your driver informs you that they don't have a meter / don't use their meter, always negotiate your trip price before departing (again, you can ask a local what would be fair). Most official taxi companies use red vehicles, so keep that in mind before you jump into someone's car claiming to be a taxi (at the airport the taxis are sometimes orange).

There is, however, another mode of taxi-like transportation, a ride share option called a "collectivo." A private driver offers shared rides around the city or even between cities, charging a quarter or less of the fee you would pay in a taxi alone. Think of it as a kind of Costa Rican Uber. You'll know a collectivo when you see one - the driver usually cruises by popular places like bus terminals, bus stops, ferry docks, and airports (just like an Uber driver might), casually yelling their destination out of the window or simply yelling the word "collectivo."

Pro tip: use a landmark to describe your destination to your taxi driver, as many locations in Costa Rica don't have an exact address. And just a quick reminder - don't ever let your taxi driver change your mind about your chosen destination. This is likely a scam.

Flights

There are many daily flights all throughout Costa Rica, and for the most part, they're quick and cheap (domestic flights start around $60USD). That is if you don't have a lot of luggage! If you're traveling light (10 pounds or 4.5 kilos or less), flights are affordable. Any more luggage than that, and you will start to incur heavy baggage fees, and your cheap flight will suddenly get very expensive.

Rental Cars

Whether this is a great option or not really depends on your experience as a driver, how comfortable you are driving in a foreign country with sometimes confusing signs in a foreign language, and how much money you want to spend on travel. In general, driving a rental car on your first few holidays in Costa Rica is not really recommended. Many roads in the country are full of potholes, signage can be ambiguous, and cities are hard to navigate. I'm an excellent driver, and I speak Spanish, but I'm still hesitant to rent a car here. Plus, it can be very expensive.

Uber

Yes! Many a traveler will be extremely delighted to find that Costa Rica does indeed have Uber ever since it was introduced to the country in 2015. Unfortunately, it's still in its growing phrase, and as of 2020, Ubers are mostly only available in San José and its surrounding metropolitan area. You might be able to find one in some of the larger cities of Liberia - though it's unlikely at this point, it can't hurt to check! Pro tip: use a landmark to describe your destination, as many locations in Costa Rica don't have an exact address.

Six Things You Need to Know Before Visiting

If you are a first-time traveler to Costa Rica, there are a few important things you should know before you plan and pack for your grand adventure. Here are six of my best travel tips - you can thank me later!

Currency

The national currency of Costa Rica is the colón (₡), or plural, colones. Colones are available in coins that range from five colones to 500 colones, and polymer bills that range from 1,000 colones to 50,000 colones. Polymer bills were introduced nationwide for the purpose of preventing the high counterfeiting rate of the previous cotton-paper bills. The exchange rate can fluctuate daily, but in general, 1 U.S. dollar converts to roughly 500-600 colones (as of 2020).

U.S. dollars are widely accepted at many establishments in the most popular, touristic areas of the country, and even in many places off the beaten track. The banking system in Costa Rica has vastly improved over the years; there are many ATMs and banks scattered throughout the country, and the majority of them offer cash withdrawals in either colones or U.S. dollars.

However, there are a few things to remember that will help make your vacation stress-free and safe:

> Be prepared to wait in line inside of the bank, and make sure you bring your passport for any transactions inside of the bank. The service may be personable and friendly, but there is almost always a long line.

> It's never guaranteed that your preferred destination will accept anything other than Costa Rican colones,

so it's always a wise decision to keep local currency with you at all times.

Public transportation, for instance, will only accept colones. Make sure you have small bills; they do not always have change for larger bills.

If a business does accept U.S. currency, many will still not accept U.S. bills over $20 dollars, especially in rural areas. If you withdraw cash that comes in $50 dollar bills, try to break them in the city before heading out to the country.

It's wise to use U.S. currency only where you are able to use a calculator to convert the price from colones, or if the cashier is working off of a computer system, to ensure a fair conversion. For smaller exchanges such as taxi rides and buses, for example, it's always better to use colones.

If you choose to change your foreign currency into colones, don't do it at the airport - they generally have the worst conversion fees. Try a local bank instead.

Banco de Costa Rica, or BCR, is the only bank that does not charge foreign transaction fees for withdrawals from their ATMs. Yay for no fees!

Credit cards are widely accepted across the country.

Traveler's checks are not widely accepted, so I don't recommend using them.

Tipping

Tipping in Costa Rica is generally not as customary as it is in some countries such as the United States. While most travelers do choose to leave a tip for selected services because of their low wage rate, many Costa Ricans are paid, and/or because they appreciated the customer service or meal, it is absolutely up to you to decide. The word for "tip" in Spanish is "propina."

While tipping can be for any service, like a taxi ride, haircut, or massage, this question seems to arise most for travelers when in a restaurant or bar setting. If you are dining in an upscale restaurant or bar, you may want to check your bill or ask your server if they have already added gratuity to your check. Smaller and more casual establishments do not do this. A good rule of thumb for budget travel is leaving a few 500 colones coins if you appreciated the service, meal, or drinks. If you can afford it, leaving a 10% tip is considered very polite and greatly appreciated for local workers.

Important note for dining out - keep in mind that in Costa Rica, your server or bartender will usually not bring your check until you ask for it. This is not bad service; it is their way of not rushing you.

Electric Voltage & Outlets

There are two main differences in using electricity around the world that are important to know for us world travelers: voltage and electrical outlets (also known as sockets). Voltage is the measure of electric pressure or strength. Electrical outlets (or sockets) are where you plug in your mobile phone to recharge every day, and they are a little different in each country.

A quick check now might potentially save you some trouble later, as each country has different types of electrical outlets and voltages, and chances are good that your country's specifications do not perfectly match Costa Rica's. What will happen if you try to plug in a device with the wrong voltage? You might see a flash and smoke, and something might melt. What will happen if you try to plug a device into the wrong kind of outlet? Well, you won't be able to, because it won't fit.

Honestly, I recommend bringing a universal adapter and converter with you on any travel adventure, whether or not you "match," just in case. You never know which country's airport you might connect in, or how long your layover will be, and it's always nice to be able to charge up before jumping back on the plane. In any case, it's still a smart idea to read up on where your country stands in the lists of different types of voltages/outlets around the world that I've compiled in APPENDIX B (at the end of this book). And then, buy a universal adapter and converter, anyway!

As you can see from the appendix, it's a real mixed bag, so your safest bet is to just go ahead and buy a universal adapter and converter.

Healthcare

One of my favorite convenient aspects of traveling in Costa is their excellent healthcare system. It's considered to be one of the best healthcare systems in all of Latin America (Mexico, Central America, South America), so you can rest easy on your travels here, knowing that no matter what medical need you have, you will be in good hands. Costa Rica has consistently ranked #1 in the world on the Happy Planet Index, a project that collects comprehensive data from every country in the world and measures what they refer to as "sustainable wellbeing for all," or nations are doing at achieving long, happy, sustainable lives. Costa Rica also has an impressive life expectancy of 80.1 years... for reference, the United States life expectancy is 78.6. How? Well, a large part of the answer is surely their competent, accessible, and affordable healthcare system.

Before you leave home, however, you will want to consider your travel insurance options for your Costa Rican vacation and purchase coverage based on your projected needs during your stay. Costa Rica has two healthcare systems: a universal healthcare system run by the government, and a private healthcare system. You can join one of these options for your stay, or you can select an international insurance plan.

Choose Your Coverage Plan

Here are some good questions to ask yourself in order to choose the best plan for you:

> Does your current insurance plan cover your travel in Costa Rica?

> Do you plan on going on any big hikes, adventure activities, or extreme sports while you are in Costa Rica?

How long will you be traveling to Costa Rica?

Based on your answers to these questions, you can choose from the following coverage options for your travels.

Costa Rica's government healthcare system. The Caja Costarricense de Seguro Social, often simply referred to as the "Caja," will cover visitors for a small monthly fee based on your income. This coverage grants you treatment in designated public facilities in Costa Rica throughout your stay.

Costa Rica's private healthcare system. The Instituto Nacional de Seguros will cover visitors for an affordable premium and offers a 5% discount for families. This coverage grants you access to the private network of doctors and hospitals in Costa Rica throughout your stay. Here is an example of a premium, according to Casa Presidencial, a local news outlet: a 45-year-old visiting for two weeks can expect to pay $9.40 per day (about $132 total).

International health insurance. If you already have health insurance, talk to your provider about your options for international travel. If you don't have health insurance (yes, there are still some rebels out there - like me), a quick search online will show a great selection of affordable travel health insurance options. No matter what route you choose, be sure to choose a plan that includes coverage for emergency medical evacuation and repatriation.

Even though Costa Rican healthcare is high quality and constantly being improved upon, the costs are far lower than you would find in many first world countries. For example, you might pay as little as $20-35USD for a healthcare service in Costa Rica that would cost you $100USD in the United States. A large percentage of Costa Rican doctors speak English (especially in private practices), and many of them have even received part or all of their medical training in the United States, Canada, or Europe.

Large Private Hospitals

There are three large, private hospitals that most expatriates use: CIMA hospital in Escazú, Clínica Bíblica in San José, and Hospital La Católica in San José-Guadalupe. All these facilities are in and around the capital of the country, San José.

In this private system, you can pay cash or use insurance, including some policies from the U.S. and Europe, international policies, and insurance from Costa Rican companies.

Crime & Safety

Costa Rica is considered to be the safest travel destination in Central America, and one of the safest budget travel destinations in the world. There are many reasons for this. It was at least due in part to the dissolution of their military on December 1, 1948. Since that day, Costa Rica has remained peaceful in terms of both civil and international warfare. The lack of government spending on the machinations of war means that those funds are instead spent elsewhere, for example, on infrastructure and education. Costa Rica enjoys an infrastructure system that is better than any other Central American country, with a reasonably good education system as well. Local residents can earn a decent wage in comparison to their Central American neighbors. Crime rates are relatively low compared to other countries in Central and South America.

Crime Rates

Having said all of that, nowhere in the world is perfect, and Costa Rica is still growing as a nation. Violent crime and sexual assault are not common but do happen; non-violent theft and burglary are far more common, but still reasonably infrequent. In all of my travels in Costa Rica, I have never had a problem. That is not to say that crimes do not happen.

But if you employ a traveler's caution, do your research, and have a little luck on your side, you shouldn't experience any problems, either. Your best protection is always prevention by educating yourself prior to travel.

High-Threat Areas

According to the U.S. Department of State, San José is a high-threat location for crime. There are many wonderful attractions to consider visiting in San José, so don't cross it off your list just yet! Your best bet is to exercise increased caution while visiting the nation's vibrant capital city and metropolitan area, especially if you are a solo traveler and/or female.

The few times I have felt unsafe in Costa Rica have mainly been when changing bus terminals in the bigger cities of San José, Liberia, and Limón. The neighborhoods that several of the major bus terminals are located in have high rates of crime, so it's wise to exercise increased caution in transit. If you have to walk a few blocks from one bus terminal to the other (common in the bigger cities), call a taxi or an Uber to get to the next terminal - who cares if it's only a few blocks away. Your safety and sense of well-being are worth it.

Other high-risk areas noted by the U.S. Department of State

include central Limón, Liberia, the Desamparados neighborhood in San Rafael, and especially the Pavas and Hospital neighborhoods in San José due to their high crime rates.

Safety Tips

Just like you would for a vacation in any country, follow the golden traveler rules. The phone number you can dial for help in any kind of emergency in Costa Rica is 911 (just like in the United States).

Plan your trip wisely before you leave home: do your research, learn about the place you are going, and the safe practices for each area

Don't walk alone at night

Never become inebriated with strangers

Don't flash your valuables, wads of cash, or inappropriate skin

Don't let anyone watch your luggage for you

Do not let your taxi driver ever change your mind about your destination - this likely a scam

Download the Uber app before you leave home (yes, Costa Rica has Uber in some places!)

Email a picture of your passport to yourself, in case you lose your passport/phone

Only stay in accommodations with good reviews

Look busy at bus stations to avoid scammers (even if you're lost)

Never turn your back on the ocean

Always be wary of rip currents and tides (ask a local)

Typical Food and Drinks of Costa Rica

Traditional Costa Rican food will usually feature one or more of the following: rice, beans, tortillas, eggs, fried plantains, grilled chicken, beef, or fish, fresh tropical fruit, and fresh vegetables. Western fare such as hamburgers, French fries, sandwiches, and many international cuisines such as Thai food and Italian pizza can be found almost everywhere in the more popular, touristic areas.

However, the more you get off the beaten track, the more likely you are looking at a casado plate (a combination of rice, beans, plantains, vegetables, and grilled meat) or a gallo pinto plate (special rice and pinto bean meal, often accompanied by a few corn tortillas and an egg for breakfast or grilled meat for lunch) for most meals - and this is great news! Because the local food will almost always be cheaper, and once you have a casado or gallo pinto, you'll probably fall in love with Costa Rica even more. Though the food may seem "plain" to some travelers, it is hearty, filling, tasty, and often made by a Costa Rican grandmother - so you know it's good. Gallo pinto and casados have easily become some of my favorite foods from traveling around the world. Gallo pinto, at a glance, sounds fairly simple and bland. But intoxicatingly bland, like mashed potatoes - it is not just rice and beans. There's a secret way that locals make it, with a special vegetable stock, and I have to admit that it's my all-time favorite post-surf breakfast! If you're looking to make friends with the locals, ask someone how to make gallo pinto. 9 times out of 10, you'll get a detailed description of their personal recipe, a new friend, and sometimes even an invite to dinner.

Local Restaurants

The most traditional and common restaurant is called a "Soda," which is roughly translated to a diner, or a simple little family eatery offering a few variations of the same dishes. For the most part, "Soda" restaurants are no-frills and cozy in the familiar sense, and they almost always offer the most (and best) food for the lowest price. Plus, you're guaranteed to be supporting a local Costa Rican family by eating your meals at a Soda. Eating local is always a wonderful and tasty way to support the local economy.

Cost of Food

Compared to other countries nearby, food in Costa Rica is considered to be a little bit pricey. If you eat out, you're looking at $4 to $7 U.S. dollars for breakfast, $5 to $9 for lunch, $10 to $15 for dinner - and these are budget prices. Your best bet as a budget traveler is to eat at the Sodas often, shop at the local grocery store for lower priced items such as rice, beans, oatmeal, vegetables, cereal, eggs, and coffee, and stay in accommodations that offer a kitchen, such as hostels (featuring bunk rooms and a shared kitchen) and cabinas (small studios or cottages that have a small kitchenette) so that you can cook your own meals and make your own coffee.

This is a great way to make new friends, too if you stay at a hostel! I've been invited to impromptu "family" dinners at the hostel and made many new friends through conversations in the kitchen. One thing every culture has in common is the love of food and of sharing that with your family, friends, or whoever is closest to you.

Alcohol

On the topic of consumption, one of the most popular alcoholic drinks in Costa Rica is a distilled local liquor called "guaro." Guaro is made from sugarcane and can be likened to white rum, but the flavor is very different and completely unique to this special spirit. The famous brand of guaro that can be found on every grocery store shelf is a brand called "Cacique Guaro" with an image of a chieftain on the label. Fun fact: before the Spaniards arrived in Costa Rica, many indigenous groups of people lived peacefully under the rule of a powerful chief. They referred to their native chief respectfully as "Cacique." So, it really is the liquor for royalty! This a fun gift to take back home to share.

If a local offers you a sip of Cacique or guaro, you have made a new friend! Give it a try; it's a very smooth liquor. If you get a chance to try a "shot" of "chile guaro" (guaro mixed with a special hot sauce), don't pass it up - it's delicious, peppery, and not nearly as intense as it sounds! It's closer to a spicy V8 or tomato juice than actual hot sauce. I loved the unique flavor.

What to Pack for Your Costa Rican Adventure

Now that you know when the best times of year to visit are, and the history of the wonderful country you will be visiting, and how to stay safe, and all of the amazing fun activities to partake in, and where to stay, and how to travel around... now the big question is, what to wear?! And the answer is very simple: not much! Unless you plan on a big hike to a high altitude summit like Cerro Chirripó (the highest mountain in Costa Rica with an altitude of 12,533ft / 3821m) with a stay in a quaint little mountain town like San Gerardo de Rivas in its foothills or a visit to the cloud forests of lovely Monteverde, you really won't need to bring much warm clothing at all. If you plan on visiting during the green / rainy season, of course, you'll want to make sure to bring quality waterproof outerwear (Goretex is best), and if you plan to spend any time in the city's capital, San José, you might want to bring a dressier outfit or two. Below are a few lists of the essentials you'll want to pack for your Costa Rican trip, no matter where you plan to visit.

Digital Pack List: 5 Items You Should Not Leave Home Without

Never heard of this one, have you? But there are a few digital items you need to "pack" before leaving home to save yourself a world of inconvenience later. Here are my top five.

1. Download Uber, a rideshare app, if you don't already have it.

2. Download WhatsApp, a messaging app, if you don't already have it - almost everyone in Costa Rica uses WhatsApp, because when you use it with Wi-Fi, there is no cost.

3. Take a picture of your passport/insurance/any other important documents and email them to yourself in case of an emergency (like, you lose your passport, phone, wallet, or luggage).

4. Search online for a few of the taxi company phone numbers in each of the different cities you will be visiting, and enter them into your phone's contacts.

5. Download Waze (most commonly used in Costa Rica), or another GPS app like Maps.Me or Google Maps. Before you embark on any adventures on your holiday, enter your destination in the app and download the directions before you leave, just in case you need them offline.

Everyday Pack List: 28 Items You Will Need Everywhere

No matter where you go in Costa Rica, you'll definitely want to pack the following to have the best, safest, most fun, comfortable budget vacation possible.

1. **Athletic footwear**. Either hiking boots or sturdy running shoes for hikes and trails. If you plan on doing a serious hike, be sure to bring footwear with solid ankle support.

2. **Sandals**. Your best bet is to bring a pair of flip flops for the beach and comfortable walking sandals for all things casual (which will be most of your days). If you want, you can bring a nicer pair for outings to restaurants, bars, or clubs.

Costa Rica is very, very casual (unless you're in the capital city), and sandals are the shoe du jour.

3. **Water Shoes**. These can come in handy if you're visiting waterfalls, which can sometimes be slippery. Plus, if it's the rainy season, you'll be happy to have shoes that can comfortably get wet! I don't personally bring them, but I know many travelers who do.

4. **Swimsuits**. All types of swimwear are acceptable in Costa Rica, and you will probably be in your swimsuit at least half of your trip! So it's probably smart to pack a few.

5. **Extra socks**. It's very humid almost everywhere in the country, so you might be very grateful to have a few extra pairs of dry socks for your hiking or trail adventures, or for those long, air-conditioned bus rides.

6. **Towel**. If you plan on staying at hostels or inexpensive hotels, you will need to bring your own bath towel. Plus, it can double as your towel for the beach. If you don't have that much space in your luggage, try bringing a sarong as your towel instead, or a small microfiber towel (made of hyper-evaporative material).

7. **Rain Jacket**. Even if it's not the rainy season, and you'll

be visiting drier climate areas of the country, it's still the tropics, and can rain at any time. I always bring a rain jacket just in case, no matter which part of the country I will be visiting.

8. **Light Cardigan, Flannel, or Long Sleeve Shirt**. It's unlikely you'll use it often, but you'll be glad to have it on the rare "chilly" evening, or, more likely, for an 8 hour, icy cold A.C. bus ride.

9. **Sunglasses & Hat**. The sun can be relentless here, and it's always reccomended to wear a hat and polarized sunglasses to protect your face and eyes. Make sure you choose a sunscreen that does not contain the harmful ingredient oxybenzone - this unnecessary chemical kills ocean reefs, harms aquatic life, and has already been banned in Hawai'i and other tropical destinations around the world.

10. **Rash Guard**. If you plan on partaking in any kind of water sports, you might want to bring your own rash guard as an extra layer of protection from the sun (and from your surfboard if you're surfing).

11. **Dry Bag**. If you don't have one already, this is a great item to have for traveling! It will keep your essentials dry if you go on a boat trip, hike through rivers or waterfalls, or

plan on kayaking. It's also an excellent idea to keep your electronics in here at all times on your trip to protect them from the humidity.

12. **Reusable Water Bottle**. As mentioned earlier in the book, this is one of the easiest ways to save money! You can refill your water bottle almost anywhere, just ask nicely. Plus, you're helping save the Earth by not purchasing unnecessary single use plastics.

13. **Toiletries**. Be warned, toiletries can be 3 or 4 times the price in Costa Rica, so bring your own if you are on a budget! Small containers of shampoo, conditioner, face wash, soap, tampons, and a couple of extra pairs of contact lenses, if you use these items.

14. **Sunscreen & Insect Repellent**. Bring sunscreen no matter where you are going. If you're planning on being in the jungle at all, be sure to bring your repellent, and, pro tip: DEET is the gold standard of insect repellents, but the efficacy of DEET plateaus at 25%, so there's really no need to buy repellents with higher levels of DEET.

15. **Alcohol**. If you are really on a budget and don't mind carrying around the weight, you can bring up to 5 liters of alcohol into the country to save a little bit of money - alcohol

can be expensive here.

16. **Spanish Phrasebook**. While you have already learned some great conversational Spanish words and phrases to get you started, it's always a great idea to have a phrasebook handy to communicate with locals on the fly!

17. **First Aid Kit** - You can never go wrong with a small, portable medical kit containing the essentials for minor accidents and emergencies on any travels (include at least Band-Aids, antiseptic, antibiotic ointment, absorbent compression dressing, tweezers, painkiller, gauze pad). Safety first!

18. **Pharmacy Kit**. You'll be pleasantly surprised at the convenience of Costa Rican pharmacies; they generally have anything you'll need, and often speak a little bit of English. But I still recommend bringing your own little "pharmacy" with you when you travel anywhere. I always have a couple of the following: anti-nausea, anti-diarrhea, laxative, aspirin, painkiller, sleeping pill, cold/flu day/night tablets. I rarely use them, but the few times I have were so worth it.

19. **Money Belt & Passport Holder**. This is generally the safest way to store your money and passport while traveling anywhere. While Costa Rica's crime rate is very low, it still

exists, and it's better to be safe than sorry. Even if you don't use it often, having the option is smart.

20. **Flashlight or headlamp**. It's rare that you'll need it, but you just never know! In some of the more remote towns or during storms, electricity can occasionally be unreliable. And due to the fickle nature of reality vs. planning, I've definitely been dropped off at a bus stop in the dark once or twice, for example, and was very glad to have my headlamp.

21. **Rechargeable Battery Pack**. For long journeys, hikes, or if you plan on traveling during the rainy season when electricity can be a little less reliable, a battery pack is a great bet. Actually, it's just a great idea for any trip - no more dead phone or camera battery, right when you need it most!

22. **Day Pack**. Bring a smaller tote bag or comfortable backpack for the beach, hikes, or day trips (I prefer a backpack because it's more versatile).

23. **Sealable Plastic Baggies.** A few of these always come in handy. They're great for keeping your phone or electronics dry at the beach, keeping your smaller items organized, or for bringing snacks everywhere. If you have a little extra cash, try buying reusable, lockable plastic bags! They work just as well, save you money in the end, and reduce your

plastic waste. They're awesome!

24. **Large Plastic Garbage Bags**. A great way to "give back" on your trip is to bring a trash bag with you to the beach once or twice... invite a few people from your hostel or accommodation, and take a pretty walk down the beach to pick up some rubbish.

25. **Lock**. If you will be staying at hostels, bring your own lock in case you use a locker.

26. **Earplugs**. Always a good backup for sleeping while traveling! Just in case your hotel is by a highway, or you sleep in a hostel that can be noisy late into the night, or you want to catch some zzz's on your chosen mode of transportation.

27. **Mask/Goggles, Snorkel, Fins**. It's up to you whether you'd rather rent the gear as needed, but if you plan on snorkeling a lot, you might as well BYO and save a little extra cash. At the very least, bring some goggles with you - they barely take up any space, and give you the "seeing underwater" option no matter where you go.

28. **Mace, Doorstop, Whistle**. These extra protections are more important for solo travelers, especially if you are

female, but I recommend them for anyone. I like to travel with a tiny canister of mace in my backpack in every foreign country - can't hurt, could come in handy. A whistle is even smaller but still potentially helpful in an emergency, and a doorstop provides a little extra security at night.

Green/Wet Season Pack List: 4 Extra Items

If you're traveling during the green/wet season, you will definitely want to add a couple of extra things to your pack list. A little preparation goes a long way towards making sure you have the best trip possible, rain or no rain (but probably rain).

1. **Waterproof outerwear**. Make sure your rain jacket is waterproof, not water repellent; this is a very important distinction (Goretex is a safe bet). You may also want to bring waterproof pants if you will be traveling anywhere a little cooler, such as San José, up in the mountains, or in the cloud forests.

2. **Umbrella**. Bring an umbrella if you don't want to have to wear your waterproof outer clothing all of the time.

3. **Waterproof Backpack Cover**. Most large backpacks

come with a pack cover pre-installed (check the very bottom of your bag or ask the manufacturer), but if not, you can purchase one for as little as $5USD at your local outdoor gear store.

4. **Comfortable, Quick-Dry Walking Sandals**. You might want to consider splashing out on a pair of Chaco or Keen sandals - they're super comfortable rainy season or not, and they dry quickly after getting wet. Worth it! Definitely optional, but highly recommended.

Higher Elevations Pack List: 4 Extra Items

If you're traveling to San José, the mountains, or the cloud forests, make sure to add the following to your pack list to keep you warm and cozy no matter what adventures you choose.

1. **Warm Jacket.** Depending on where you're going, a warm jacket, sweater, flannel, or fleece is a great idea to keep warm. Read a few blogs and reviews of the area to be sure.

2. **Long Pants.** Jeans, hiking pants, and leggings are all smart to pack for these locations. Ladies, be advised that leggings worn alone are not very common here.

3. **Dressy Outfit / Warm Covering**. Clothing is a little bit more formal in the capital city, so you might want to bring a nicer set of clothing, including longer bottoms and a warm covering.

4. **Warm Hat**. If you'll be at very high altitudes, bring a beanie or warm hat, and a scarf.

What NOT To Pack: 4 Items That Are Just a Waste of Space

Conversely, there are a few items that you should not bother bringing on your trip to Costa Rica. Here are a few items that may just be wasting space in your luggage if you bring them.

1. **Expensive Jewelry**. It's a very casual dress code here. And more importantly, there's no need to advertise your wealth unnecessarily and draw attention to thieves.

2. **Stilettos or High Heels**. Again, it's very casual here, and it's rare to have a smoothly paved street anywhere, so walking can be quite tricky in heels. Unless you plan on staying in San José for most of your trip and frequenting fancy places, they are probably unnecessary.

3. **Rainboots/Mudboots**. Even at the height of the rainy

season, you're better off with water shoes that take up less room in your luggage and dry out faster.

4. Leggings. Warning to the ladies: leggings are not yet considered appropriate everywhere in Costa Rica, and you will definitely be stared at. It's a probably best to completely forego them while you are in San José or inland towns just to be safe. They are, however, acceptable and even common in more casual beach towns.

The Soul of Costa Rica: Sustainability & Traveling in 2020

Now that you've almost reached the end of your trusty little Costa Rica travel guide, you should have a basic understanding of several of the more important practical parts of a Costa Rican holiday or vacation. However, there's so much more to this incredible, pocket-sized nation, and I hope you will continue to study and learn about Costa Rica's amazing culture. There is one topic, though, that would be remiss of me to neglect mentioning because it's such a huge part of Costa Rica's cultural identity.

With every new country you visit in your travels, you may notice that each culture has one or more unique chosen trademarks or defining features. I'm not talking about naturally occurring wonders of the world, like the Whale Tail in Uvita, or the perfect wave at Playa Grande (near Tamarindo) or Salsa Brava (near Puerto Limón), or the fact that this Central American nation has more humpback whales in residence than anywhere else in the world. I'm talking about something special that sets each country apart, something that was consciously chosen by its people.

For Costa Rica, many would argue that their "defining feature" is their unwavering dedication to sustainability in the past few decades. "We are declaring peace with nature," said the ambassador of Costa Rica, Mario Fernández Silva, referring to the abolition in 1958 of Costa Rica's army and the subsequent reinvestment of government spending. "We feel a strong sense of responsibility about looking after our wealth of biodiversity. Our attitude is not progressive, it is conservative. Our view is that until we know what we have, it is our duty to protect it." Or, as everyday Costa Ricans put it, "Sustainability is not a practice in Costa Rica; it is a way of life."

In modern times, when people use the word "sustainability," they are most often referring to environmental sustainability; however, the word and concept are both deeply multi-faceted. Costa Rica knows and understands this, and arguably that is why they have been so successful in implementing sustainability throughout their country in just a few short decades.

The dictionary defines "sustainable" or "sustainability" as

> *Something pertaining to a system that maintains its own viability by using techniques that allow for continual reuse of, relating to, or being a method of harvesting or using a resource so that the resource is not depleted or permanently damaged; sustainable techniques sustainable agriculture; of, or relating to a lifestyle involving the use of sustainable methods sustainable society; of, or relating to environmental science: the quality of not being harmful to the environment or depleting natural resources, and thereby supporting long-term ecological balance.*

The word sustainable or sustainability can be applied to a singular system. For example, our backyard garden might be sustainable if we designed it with permaculture practices in mind. Or in another example, our spending habits are sustainable only if we make enough money to pay for all of the things we need. But if we're looking at the concept of sustainability from a larger or higher level, say, for the governance of an entire nation, it really must encompass the whole picture, not just a single part. Some might call that "holistic" sustainability. Holistic means taking into consideration all of the parts of a system and its interactions with other systems. In its simplest form, holistic sustainability can be divided into what is known as the "three pillars of sustainability": environment, economy, and society. Each part can act independently of the others, but in order to achieve balance and growth, the parts must work and cooperate together.

In a nutshell, for the purpose of governance, holistic sustainability is all about meeting the current needs of a nation without compromising the resources needed for future generations.

We'll be focusing on environmental sustainability with a few references to economic sustainability and socio-cultural sustainability and to see how they all tie in together. I'll briefly cover a few important notes on environmental sustainability in Costa Rica, such as our roles as travelers, Costa Rica's background in moving towards some of the most ambitious sustainability goals set by any country on Earth, the various laws, regulations, processes, and programs the Costa Rican government has set in place to achieve success, and a brief overview of their progress over the past three decades.

Buckle in, it's a great story! Costa Rica's relationship with sustainability is fascinating and uplifting by turns, as we learn how this tiny Central American nation managed to rise above their struggles and become one of the most respected countries on the planet for their environmental policies. Regardless of Costa Rica's size, it is one of the world leaders in going green - and for that reason, we all have something very valuable to learn from beautiful Costa Rica.

The Background of Costa Rica's Sustainability

In 2019, Costa Rica proudly reported that it had operated on over 98% renewable energy for its fifth consecutive year, which is no small feat for a population of five million people that hosted over three million tourists in 2019. The nation is able to achieve these ambitious goals because sustainable practices are embraced and followed in every part of the country and in every industry. The concept of sustainability is woven throughout the fabric of Costa Rica's cultural traditions and passed down from generation to generation.

It wasn't always this way, though. Costa Ricans have been

working hard to return to sustainable practices and earn their place as one of the most environmentally-friendly nations on Earth.

Back in the 1940s, more than 75% of Costa Rican land was covered in thick forests and verdant jungles. By the time 1987 rolled around, that number had dropped steeply to about 20%. Why? The change was largely due to the world's economical climate attitude, which unfortunately still prevails today in most modern nations: the idea that undeveloped lands such as natural fields, forests, and jungles are "unproductive lands," as opposed to developed land that is considered "productive land." Thankfully, the leadership in Costa Rica began to realize the error of this logic back in the early 1990s. Their soils were depleted. Their waterways were polluted. The quality of drinkable water and breathable air was degenerating. Desertification and greenhouse gases were on the rise. They realized their most precious assets as a nation were, in fact, their natural resources.

Thankfully, Costa Rica was already very comfortable in blazing new paths. As mentioned in our history chapter, the government formally abolished the National Army of Costa Rica in 1948, an act which was preserved for all time as a permanent addition to the Costa Rican constitution. At the time of abolishment, their primary purpose was to embrace and promote peace as a fundamental constitutional value. Their reasoning was that the country did not want to adopt the limited concept of peace that only exists in the absence of war. It's difficult to say if anyone knew at the time how far-reaching the consequences of this landmark decision would be (Costa Rica was the first country in the world to abolish their military, followed in 1989 by their neighbor, Panama), but what it meant for the country and its people was a redirection of military spending into crucial investment into developing programs for improvement in the education, health, and environment sectors of Costa Rican society.

The new policy also promoted conflict resolution via non-military means and allowed the nation to achieve one of the highest living standards in all of Central America. Thanks to Panama following suit in demilitarizing their own country, Costa Rica also has one of the "world's safest borders" with their neighbor. The subsequent growth stemming from these implemented changes has made all the difference in setting this nation apart from any of their neighbors, and indeed, from most of the world.

So, back to the early 1990s, when the leaders of Costa Rica realized another big change was needed as they watched their forests, jungles, clean air, wildlife, and drinkable water dwindle rapidly before their eyes. Fortunately, they had the earned experience of revolutionary change already, in addition to available funding (from demilitarization) for their biggest project yet: making Costa Rica green again. The government leaders undertook some very serious due diligence into the economic, socio-cultural, and environmental benefits of restoring and maintaining healthy ecosystems. In other words, they began to look closely at how to make their entire country as sustainable as possible while supporting the local economy. They established national parks, encouraged organic agriculture to all citizens and businesses, implemented conservation policies, and began to promote ecotourism.

Ecotourism, defined loosely as "responsible travel to natural areas that conserves the environment, sustains the well-being of the local people and involves education of both staff and guests," was still a brand new concept in the 1990s. Costa Rica was blazing trails again, and the country quickly began to see the benefits to their environment and economy. The secret, the government realized, was to ensure holistic sustainability was being observed. This led to profitable practices that bolstered the economy while simultaneously preserving natural resources.

In 1998, in the midst of their ongoing success, and in response to the United Nations (UN) Convention on

Biological Diversity, Costa Rica took it a step further and drafted their Costa Rica Biodiversity Law. The new law permanently enforced Costa Rica's adopted environmental principles and embraced the three objectives of the recent UN Convention: conservation of biodiversity, sustainable use of resources, and the fair and equitable sharing of the benefits arising from the utilization of genetic resources. The new Costa Rican law was held up as a model for other nations to follow and still is considered today a shining example of what a country can achieve in preserving its biodiversity.

Costa Rica also established a national biodiversity commission made up of scientists, indigenous representatives, and civil servants, who propose environmental policies to the government while promoting "green" education for the people of Costa Rica and the tourists that visit every year. Thanks to these forward-thinking practices, today, the amount of Costa Rica's forested land has increased to well over 50% of the total landmass of the country.

Our Incredibly Important Role as Travelers

Our actions as travelers play a very important role in all of this. Every choice we make in our daily lives as a consumer has a lasting impact on our surroundings - that's as true as it is for when we are at home, as it is for when we travel. Every dollar you spend, and every step you take, has the direct power to make a difference in the culture you visit. As one traveler smartly put it, "deciding to travel sustainably is kind of like taking the Hippocratic oath - first, do no harm." When you purchase a product (was it handmade locally? Or imported from China?), decide to eat at a certain restaurant (is it a local restaurant? Or a global chain?), choose your type of transportation, rent accommodation, book or plan activities - all of these things make a difference to the culture you're visiting.

Our choices influence our environment. We vote all day, every day, with the dollars we spend and the selections we make. Being conscious of this is the first and most important step in striving to be a sustainable traveler. A vacation or holiday is often something we dream of and plan for days, weeks, months, or even years. A few extra minutes of research can mean the world of difference in traveling sustainably and supporting your new favorite tropical destination! Here are a few simple tips to being a sustainable traveler that I've learned through my own travels and through extensive research.

Bring a reusable water bottle everywhere. I like to use a Hydro Flask (or any type of container that retains temperature) - that way, my water bottle can double as a coffee cup when I visit a cafe or as an icy drink holder for a trip to the beach.

Use water sparingly. A lot of the places you visit might not mention it because it looks bad for business, but water is a precious commodity, and you would be doing them a great service by shortening your shower by even a few minutes, turning the tap off while you brush your teeth, or reusing your hotel towels.

Save electricity. It might seem like a small gesture when you turn off the light or air conditioner when leaving the room, but the tally of energy saved at the end of a year of doing so is ginormous! Imagine if every traveler did that.

Support local. Every chance you get, support a local business instead of an international chain! Not only will your handmade souvenirs, delicious meals and drinks, and cozy accommodations be more authentic and make for a great memory - but you will more than likely make some wonderful new local friends in the process, too.

Respect the culture. No matter where you travel, a few

respectable practices are universal: learn a few phrases in the local language, dress appropriately where/when relevant, ask before taking a photo. A little thoughtfulness goes a long way.

Only leave your footprints. It goes without saying that you, a thoughtful traveler, would never litter! But you can also take precautions to not hike off-trail, disturb wildlife, touch historical artifacts, or alter the landscape in any way (lookin' at you, rock cairn builders! It's fun to create art, but it's not ok if it isn't your land to change). You can also choose to partake in fun activities that don't require much, if any, fossil fuel - like hiking, cycling, kayaking, horseback riding, snorkeling, etc.

Give back. This is not for everyone, of course, because sometimes, when you only have a week or two to vacation, you are understandably there to just unwind and relax. But if you do find you have a few extra hours or even a couple of days in your vacation schedule, you can easily find ways to give back to the local community by doing a quick internet search or simply asking a local. You can join a beach clean or create your own, which is my personal favorite. At least once on my trip, I like to bring a big trash bag with me to the beach and pick up any rubbish. I've found many new friends this way, as people are likely to join in if you offer a friendly smile and wave. You could also volunteer at a local school or community center, help plant trees, or a myriad of other activities that benefit the local community. Costa Rica is especially known for its many groups, projects, and organizations around the country offering opportunities such as these to any traveler or a tourist wishing to give back. A quick search online will show a multitude of options.

The Many Sustainable Programs in Costa Rica

Costa Rica has so many programs aimed at sustainability that it would almost be easier to list what they don't have! For example, the nation collects funds from a car stamp duty, energy fees, and a fuel tax, and funnels the money into biodiversity protection and managing natural reserves. Or, in another example, Costa Rican landowners are actually paid to protect and preserve any old-growth forests and to plant new trees on their properties. Here is a very short list of Costa Rica's many sustainability programs.

Certification for Sustainable Tourism (CST). This program has a complex system that basically measures the sustainability of local businesses and gives them a rating and then makes that information and rating available to the public - giving consumers the power to make educated purchases.

Bandera Azul Ecológica (Blue Ecological Flag) Program. This program not only awards the "Blue Flag" to communities across the country who meet certain sustainability requirements, but it also incentivizes them to do so and provides them with environmental education, waste management, and even comprehensive health care plans.

Payments for Environmental Services (PES) Program. As mentioned earlier, this program actually pays landowners who adopt healthy forest management practices that include maintaining clean water and preserving biodiversity. The program was created in the early 1990s to help combat deforestation. This is an incredible example of money being invested in natural resources while providing direct financial support for the community.

The National Emergency Commission. This program is a branch of the Costa Rican government that has many important functions: it coordinates risk prevention and emergency responses while raising awareness of the risk of disasters and providing emergency response education (to name a few).

The Sport & Recreational Hunting Ban

In 2012, Costa Rica banned sport hunting, or hunting purely for recreation, becoming the first country in Central America to do so. Violators can face time in prison or heavy fines. Prior to the law being passed, illegal hunting tours for tourists often targeted rare and endangered species of local animals such as the puma, jaguar, and even parrots. Local residents are still allowed to hunt and fish non-endangered species, as it is a form of sustenance for many. It's laws like these that help contribute greatly to the overall picture of sustainability in Costa Rica.

A Surplus of "Green" Energy

As mentioned earlier, Costa Rica has been running on over 98% renewable energy since 2014. Most of this green energy, about 67%, is generated by hydropower (power derived from the energy of falling or fast-running water). The power generated by wind makes up another 17%. Geothermal power sources bring in another 13%, and the remaining power is a combination of solar panels, biomass, and other renewable energy sources.

Well, guess what? Costa Rica is now producing so much renewable energy that it has more than it needs! In 2015, the Costa Rican Electricity Institute (ICE) began to sell the country's surplus of energy to its neighbors through a channel called the Central American Regional Electricity Market. Honduras, Panama, Nicaragua, El Salvador, and Guatemala all benefit from this arrangement by having access to affordable, renewable energy. And Costa Rica benefits in a major way from their efforts, too: as of 2019, the nation had earned over $180 million by selling their surplus energy.

Another unique feature of Costa Rica's approach to renewable energy is its concept of "universal access." Astonishingly, all Costa Ricans living in both rural and urban areas have access to "green" electricity generated by renewable sources. Thanks to their abundant natural resources and wise investments, the country is able to provide clean energy to the entire population, joining the likes of far wealthier countries such as Switzerland, Germany, and Iceland, in showing the rest of the world how to continue to enjoy the wonders of electricity without polluting our earth, water, and air.

Lofty Goals: Carbon Neutral by 2050

What makes Costa Rica's example of sustainability so admirable is their determination to be the best, and always looking for new ways to improve. To that end, they've made another lofty goal: to be completely carbon neutral by the time 2050 rolls around. Even though they're winning the race in many aspects of sustainability, they still have a long way to go before being fully sustainable: the country's entire transportation system is still running on fossil fuels. This will probably be one of their most difficult obstacles yet, but if their track record is anything to go by, Costa Rica will step up to the challenge with the grace, conviction, single-mindedness, and strength of will we've all come to love.

There's a lot riding on this new goal of theirs in the global sense as well. If they reach their goal of becoming a completely carbon-neutral nation, they will be the first country on Earth to do so, paving the way for countless others. And you, dear traveler, can play your part too, as you enjoy this lovely country and its endless beauty.

Appendix A

Indigenous Languages Spoken in Costa Rica

Cabécar language (.20%). Spoken by the people of the Talamanca mountain range and the Southern Pacific region. Cabécar is the sister language to Bribri, both belonging to the Isthmic branch of the Chibchan language family.

Bribri language (.24%). Spoken on the Atlantic slopes of the country, sharing some territory with the Cabécar language with which it is closely related. Bribri is the only indigenous language currently taught in Costa Rican universities. Together, Bribri and Cabécar form the Viceitic subgroup of Chibchan languages.

Maléku language (.017%). Spoken only by about 800 individuals living in the north-eastern Alajuela Province. Also known as Guatoso, Maléku belongs to the Votic branch of the Chibchan language family.

Guaymí language (.11%). Spoken in indigenous territories in the southeast of Puntarenas Province, on both sides of the Costa Rican-Panamanian border. Together, Guaymí and Buglere belong to the Guaymic subgroup of the Chibchan languages. Guaymí is also known as Ngäbere or Movere.

Buglere language (% unknown). Spoken in the southeastern part of the Puntarenas Province, very close to the border of Panama. Also known as Bokotá, a slightly different dialect. Buglere is similar to Guaymí and spoken in many of the same areas.

Teribe language (% unknown, nearly extinct). Spoken in the Puntarenas region near the Térraba River, Teribe is also known in Costa Rica as Térraba or Brorán. Teribe is a Spanish version of Tjer Di ("River of the Grandmother"), the native name for Térraba River.

Boruca language (% unknown, nearly extinct). Spoken solely in The Boruca Indigenous Reservation, located in the Puntarenas Province in southwestern Costa Rica (a few miles from the Térraba river). Boruca is also known as Brunca or Brunka.

Other Minority Languages Spoken in Costa Rica

French (.7%). There are many French residents and visitors in Costa Rica.

Portuguese (.3%). There are many Portuguese residents and visitors in Costa Rica.

German (.3%). There are many German residents and visitors in Costa Rica.

U.S. Mennonite/Quaker English (% unknown, quite small). Spoken by a group of Mennonite, or Quaker, immigrants from the U.S. who continued to speak very old-fashioned English when the rest of the USA modernized its English, and even after they moved to Costa Rica in the 1950s. They use words like "thou" instead of "you."

U.S. Mennonite/Quaker Plautdietsch (% unknown, quite small). Spoken only by a few residents in Monteverde. Plautdietsch is also known as Mennonite Low German or a Low Prussian dialect of East Low German with Dutch influence.

Costa Rican Sign Language (.027%). Spoken by deaf persons throughout the country, and their family and friends. Costa Rican Sign Language is also referred to as "Lenguaje de Senas de Costa Rica" or LESCO.

Appendix B

Is My Country's Voltage Compatible with Costa Rican Voltage?

Costa Rica uses 110 to 120 volt, 60-hertz electricity. The countries listed below use a voltage compatible with Costa Rican voltage; however, the countries in bold use multiple types of voltages, so you will still need to check the voltage of your device before plugging it in if you live in one of the countries in bold.

Countries that use a voltage that is compatible with Costa Rican voltage:

American Samoa	Anguilla	Aruba	Bahamas	Barbados
Belize	Bermuda	Bolivia	Brazil	The British Virgin Islands
Canada	Cayman Islands	Colombia	Cuba	Curaçao
Dominican Republic	Ecuador	El Salvador	French Polynesia	Guam
Guatemala	Guayana	Haiti	Honduras	Jamaica
Japan	Liberia	Libya	Madagascar	Mexico

Montserrat	Morocco	Nicaragua	North Korea	Palau
Panama	Puerto Rico	St. Kitts and Nevis	Suriname	Taiwan
Trinidad & Tobago	United States	U.S. Virgin Islands	Venezuela	

Is My Plug Compatible With Costa Rican Electrical Outlets?

Costa Rica uses the 2-pronged, flat type of electrical outlet (known as "Type A"). The countries listed in the paragraph below use plugs that are compatible with Costa Rican Type A outlets; however, the countries in bold use multiple types of electrical outlets, so you will still need to check your device's plug type if you live in one of the countries in bold.

Countries that use plugs compatible with Type A outlets

American Samoa	Anguilla	Antigua & Barbuda	Aruba	Bahamas	Barbados
Belize	Bermuda	Bolivia	The British Virgin Islands	Cambodia	Canada
Cayman	China	Colombia	Cuba	Curaçao	Dominica

Islands					n Republic
Ecuador	El Salvador	French Polynesia	Guam	Guatemala	Guyana
Haiti	Honduras	Indonesia	Jamaica	Japan	Lebanon
Liberia	Mexico	Micronesia	Montserrat	Nicaragua	Niger
North Korea	Palau	Panama	Peru	Philippines	Puerto Rico
St. Kitts and Nevis	Suriname	Taiwan	Thailand	Trinidad & Tobago	United States
U.S. Virgin Islands	Venezuela	Vietnam	Yemen		

All Other Countries - Voltage

For travelers from any countries other than those listed above, you will likely need an adapter and/or transformer for your electrical devices, as the electric voltage in other countries is normally around 220 to 240 volts. The exception to the rule is that these days, many laptops and mobile phone chargers have voltage adapters built-in to withstand anywhere from 100 to 240 voltage. However, this is not true for all laptops and mobile phone chargers, so be sure to check yours.

All Other Countries - Electrical Outlets

For travelers from any countries other than those listed above, you will need an adapter and/or transformer for your electrical devices, as the electrical outlets/plugs in other countries vary widely and will not fit your electrical device plugs.

Made in United States
Orlando, FL
07 February 2022

14569884R00109